"Purpose is firmly on the corporate agenda. T
a company than contributing to human wellbei
look at what this means in practice, and show:
wisely adopted, can be an inspirational force for _____ ___ leaders."

Dame Polly Courtice, Director of the University of
Cambridge Institute for Sustainability

"It's good to see such a direct challenge to the stale world of Corporate Social Responsibility. *The Wellbeing Purpose* is well-researched, well-written, and well-judged, and I suspect that more companies are already re-thinking their obligations in terms of their ultimate social purpose, and their true responsibilities for both staff and employees."

Jonathon Porritt, Founder Director, Forum for the Future

The Wellbeing Purpose

In a turbulent world of geopolitical change, declining trust in institutions and increasing scrutiny of companies, the big question facing leaders is: what difference does business make? Lots of companies talk about social impact, but few have defined what it really means. This book sets out a more human form of capitalism with people at its heart.

The Wellbeing Purpose is the first book that explains how companies can make life better across their value chains, from sourcing raw materials to innovating, marketing and selling products and services. This book is a blueprint for raising life satisfaction for all those touched by a business – suppliers, employees, communities and consumers. It sets out the steps for any organization to create profits (wealth creation) while simultaneously making life better (wellbeing enhancement).

Drawing on his experience as a political adviser and business consultant, Hardyment takes us on a journey across the global footprint of business. There are some startling findings along the way. Case studies from pioneering firms and the latest scientific research are used to explain how any organization can source, make and market products that create wealth and wellbeing. This is a manifesto for business to profit through helping more people to realize the good life.

Richard Hardyment has spent over a decade advising companies on responsible business practices and sustainability. He is a director at Corporate Citizenship, a global management consultancy. He was previously a political advisor in Westminster for a UK political party and senior strategic advisor at Forum for the Future.

The Wellbeing Purpose

How Companies Can Make Life Better

Richard Hardyment

Routledge
Taylor & Francis Group

LONDON AND NEW YORK

First published 2019
by Routledge
2 Park Square, Milton Park, Abingdon, Oxon OX14 4RN

and by Routledge
711 Third Avenue, New York, NY 10017

Routledge is an imprint of the Taylor & Francis Group, an informa business

British Library Cataloguing-in-Publication Data
A catalogue record for this book is available from the British Library

Library of Congress Cataloging-in-Publication Data
Names: Hardyment, Richard, author.
Title: The wellbeing purpose : how companies can make life better /
    Richard Hardyment.
Description: 1 Edition. | New York : Routledge, 2019. | Includes index.
Identifiers: LCCN 2018019584| ISBN 9781138549296 (hbk) |
    ISBN 9781138549302 (pbk) | ISBN 9781351001045 (ebk)
Subjects: LCSH: Job satisfaction. | Employee motivation. |
    Work environment.
Classification: LCC HF5549.5.J63 H297 2019 | DDC 658.3/14—dc23
LC record available at https://lccn.loc.gov/2018019584

ISBN: 978-1-138-54929-6 (hbk)
ISBN: 978-1-138-54930-2 (pbk)
ISBN: 978-1-351-00104-5 (ebk)

Typeset in Perpetua
by Swales & Willis Ltd, Exeter, Devon, UK

Printed and bound in Great Britain by
TJ International Ltd, Padstow, Cornwall

To Ada

Contents

Chapter 1

Introduction

Why happiness matters

Happiness is the meaning and purpose of life, the whole aim and end of human existence.

Aristotle (384–322 BCE)[1]

On 23 March 1768, a gentleman in a coffee shop read six words that changed our world forever. Jeremy Bentham was a child prodigy. His father told a story about how he'd found the toddler sitting at his desk, browsing a multivolume history of England. This young boy was studying Latin aged 3 and was sent up to Oxford at just 12 to study law.

On that spring morning, Bentham had returned to his alma mater to vote in parliamentary elections, as was the custom at the time. He had quickly tired of practising law, preferring instead to critique the ideas through reading and writing. Popping into a coffee shop named Harper's, on the corner by Queen's College, his attention was caught by a travelling library, tucked away at the back.

Browsing the eclectic collection of pamphlets, his eye landed on one in particular. *Essay on the First Principles of Government* had been written by a preacher named Dr Joseph Priestley. Turning its pages, Bentham made the discovery of a lifetime. Such was his shock, he was said to have yelled "Eureka!" at the top of his voice when he found these six words from Dr Priestley. What, the other drinkers in Harper's coffee shop must have wondered, had this guy just read? Bentham had stumbled upon the idea of the "greatest happiness of the greatest number."[2]

Utilitarianism, as it became known, suggests that actions should be judged by whether or not they increase or decrease our happiness. The test for everyone – governments, individuals and businesses – is the total amount of pleasure and pain that is created. Rather than following rules laid down by a god, Bentham advocated that we measure and judge our actions by their results.

Over the last 250 years, this beautifully simple idea has redefined how many think about the very purpose of life. The idea of maximizing our happiness has become a central pillar of philosophy, built on foundations laid down by Aristotle and others. Utilitarianism has transformed social welfare, and shaped political discourse and laws.

In the early twenty-first century, several governments have identified wellbeing as a new way to measure society's progress. As a complement to the traditional gross national product (GNP), policymakers have pioneered measures that have been dubbed "gross national happiness" (GNH). But we have only scratched the surface of how wellbeing might transform business.

Feeling good is a fundamental and self-evident aim of life. Happiness is what we live for. But despite all the talk of responsible and sustainable business, remarkably few companies have ever articulated their role in making us all more satisfied with life. There has been a deafening silence from the private sector about the central purpose of human existence.

This book aims to fill that void. It makes the case for wellbeing as the driving purpose of every business. A social purpose explains *why* an organization exists. Rather than vague promises about a positive role in society, the Wellbeing Purpose has a revolutionary ambition: to maximize human happiness for all those touched by a company. It places people and their feelings at the heart of the firm, whether that's farmers supplying raw materials, factory workers creating goods, or shoppers buying and consuming products and services. The Wellbeing Purpose is a blueprint for the future, a visionary moonshot, to guide research and development, procurement, marketing – in fact, all parts of the business.

A Wellthy Company

The end goal is what I call a Wellthy Company: a new type of corporation that creates wealth through wellbeing. A Wellthy Company boosts life satisfaction (wellbeing creation) and generates profits in the process (wealth creation).[3] The fruits of this wealth are shared with society through salaries for employees and business partners, taxes for governments and returns for shareholders.

When I use the term Wellthy Company, this describes a business that is reaping the benefits of the Wellbeing Purpose. While there are no fully mature Wellthy Companies today, elements can be identified in many leading businesses. The insights can be applied to any organization; they are relevant to every sector and every territory.

This isn't about doing good for its own sake. The Wellbeing Purpose can boost our world's happiness – and generate profits in the process. Enhancing life should be the social purpose of all companies because it makes great commercial sense. It's the logical next step for responsible and sustainable business in a world where more and more organizations are looking to combine profits with social value.

A focus on wellbeing can shed new light on some of the most fascinating challenges facing corporate leaders today. In a world where trust in business has collapsed, what role do companies want to play? Does paying more money to staff (and bosses) make anyone happier? Does working in a sweatshop improve quality of life or make it more miserable? Does advertising that paints a picture of what we don't have (or can't afford) undermine self-worth or inspire us to achieve more?

The science behind wellbeing

This book shows how any organization can make our world happier. When I use the term happiness, I don't mean it in some vague, fluffy sense. It's a rigorously defined and measurable indicator that is backed by decades of research. Thanks to the science of wellbeing, happiness is no longer just for the philosophers and hippies. Businesses can apply the insights to strengthen performance and improve their footprint on the world.

There is now research to show whether buying a luxury car makes us more satisfied with life, or how having a stable job or watching advertisements affects feelings of self-worth. We know whether paying people more makes them happier and what types of products do most to enhance and destroy our quality of life. This means that we can measure, quite robustly, what makes life more joyous in the short run as well as worthwhile in the round.

Over the last 30 years, well over 30,000 scholarly texts have been published on wellbeing.[4] In the last decade alone, there has been a dizzying acceleration of political interest in the topic. Politicians, policymakers and think tanks are talking about wellbeing as a new measure – for some, *the* best measure – of society's progress.

The politics of happiness

The political interest traces its roots back to 1776 in a new America. As Jeremy Bentham was floating the ideas in his own book, *Fragment on Government*, Thomas Jefferson decreed in the *Declaration of Independence* that "life, liberty and the pursuit of happiness" were the "inalienable rights" that government must protect. The most powerful critique of traditional economic measures came from Robert F. Kennedy. Just months before his tragic assassination in 1968, he proclaimed an election rally:

> Our gross national product . . . counts air pollution and cigarette advertising . . .
> It counts the destruction of the redwood and the loss of our natural wonder. . .
> and the television programs which glorify violence in order to sell toys to our
> children . . . . Yet the gross national product does not allow for the health of our
> children, the quality of their education, or the joy of their play . . . it measures
> everything, in short, except that which makes life worthwhile.[5]

Today, the governments of the UK, France, Canada and South Korea are collecting official measures of their citizens' wellbeing. Experts from Maryland and Vermont in the US, as well as Australia and the United Arab Emirates, are exploring similar metrics. As far back as 1972, the King of Bhutan announced that "gross national happiness" would become a primary aim of his country's development.[6] David Cameron, the former British Prime Minister, said that "improving our society's sense of wellbeing is, I believe, the central political challenge of our times."[7] Some, such as the happiness guru Lord (Richard) Layard, have called for wellbeing to become *the* primary objective of all government action.[8]

Far from being a sideshow, the energy and enthusiasm behind wellbeing is picking up speed. We live in a world of high uncertainty, with growing inequality, rising nationalism and geopolitical instability. How happy populations are has never been more important. Governments are trying to improve their citizens' quality of life. Isn't wellbeing what politics should ultimately be about? Given that political interest looks set to continue, it's not far-fetched to imagine that future nations could define their central political purpose not as economic growth, but as satisfaction with life for all.

These developments are highly relevant for business. Often, when governments get interested in an issue, it's only a matter of time before companies are asked: what are *you* doing about it? If we think about social changes – such as wearing seat belts, motorcycle helmets, smoking in public places or cleaning up after messy dogs[9] – it's government that has led. When governments trail-blaze, businesses are often encouraged to follow (through voluntary initiatives) or mandated to change (by regulation). But there is a more pressing reason for the business community to take wellbeing seriously: the commercial case makes it crazy to ignore.

The business opportunity

Since Jeremy Bentham was born in the middle of the eighteenth century, the global economy has grown by about 2.5% every year. This means that each generation is about a third better off than the last.[10] But despite safer workplaces, more consumer choice and rising incomes, most people are no happier with their lives. When asked to rate their satisfaction with life, where 10 represents the "best possible life" and 0 is the worst, the global average is a touch above 5. In the worst-performing countries (mostly in Sub-Saharan Africa and war-torn Syria and Afghanistan), the score is just 3.[11] That's the *average* person rating their happiness just 3 out of 10. While many people are quite content with their lot, hundreds of millions wake every day with tragically little to live for.

This human suffering is the single greatest challenge that our world faces. It is a global catastrophe. Of course, poverty, hunger, conflict, poor health and discrimination matter – but they matter because they make people miserable.

Unhappiness is an immense opportunity for forward-thinking companies. All businesses aspire to develop solutions, to bring a benefit and value to those who need it. The wellbeing economy provides a fantastic new way to create value for society. Yet, so far, too few companies have grasped this prospect. Beyond a few employee welfare schemes, the influence of companies across their supply chains and in factories, offices, shops and homes has been largely neglected.

Wellbeing is a lucrative route to wealth creation because there are countless compelling business opportunities. Disengaged employees cost American businesses an astonishing $500 billion every year in lost productivity.[12] Boosting happiness not just for staff, but right across the supply and distribution networks, can save money and dramatically increase outputs. That means lowers costs and higher margins.

Then there is the consumer. Brands that build wellbeing into their DNA can ignite long-lasting improvements to people's lives. This is absolutely not about jolly straplines; forget those smiling campaigns full of empty promises. A Wellthy Company uses the power of communications to improve health, relationships, self-esteem and all the things that raise quality of life. When a business makes life feel genuinely better, the consumer becomes the most powerful advocate that any brand could wish for. A stronger brand and higher revenues naturally flow from a focus on real human needs.

Citizens across the world are crying out for new approaches from big government as well as big business. Capitalism, in its traditional form, is floundering. In the US, the proportion of people saying they trust business to "do the right thing" is in free fall.[13] Inequality is rising and faith in the elite to solve life's problems seems to have evaporated.

As a result, we've seen Donald Trump elected to the White House and the UK vote to leave the European Union. In these populist debates, it's never the rational economic arguments – the appeal to reason – that triumphs. In what's been dubbed a post-truth world, feelings beat facts. Emotions count for more than economics. Rather than objective measures, it's how we *feel* life's going that really matters.

For businesses across the world, this should sound huge alarm bells. The old idea that companies should be left to create wealth, let it "trickle down," and we all get happier is dead. Instead, private corporations are in the dock. Frankly, many people wonder whether, amid all the cheating, profiteering and tax dodging that they hear about, companies really are doing any good. The impact of business on society matters more today than ever before – to consumers, employees, regulators and everyone else that makes or breaks a business plan. We need some truly radical ambitions from companies that improve life. The private sector needs to wake up and start measuring, managing and improving their impacts on wellbeing.

The wellbeing footprint

Every day, businesses exert an astonishing impact on life. The world's 2,000 largest companies control assets worth $170 trillion.[14] They employ millions of people and shape billions of lives through the products and services that they source, make and sell. Over the last 40 years, there has been a massive debate about what role companies should play in society.

The great untold story is about how business affects feelings about life. Some of the influences that companies create are positive, such as a steady job or a product that improves our health. But others are negative, such as human rights abuses, stress in the workplace and soul-destroying advertising.

The average person spends more of their waking hours at work than any other activity. The decisions made by business affect our relationships in the workplace, but also at home. Our daily tasks, conditions and commute shape life satisfaction quite directly. But the work setting is one tiny part of a much bigger story.

Let's take a chocolate bar by way of illustration. Beginning at the very top of the supply chain, there may be multiple imprints on happiness. The cocoa farmer has a stable job. But undignified working conditions make it unfulfilling. The chocolate factory manager jumps for joy at a promotion. But her longer hours and commute take their toll. The consumer enjoys devouring the treat. But one too many might make a health problem worse.

Companies have all sorts of positive and negative impacts on life satisfaction. The wellbeing footprint is the total picture, the costs and benefits to life across the value chain. It's complex to measure, but backed by robust science that can accurately guide decision-making.

It's no exaggeration to say that business affects how almost everyone on the planet feels about life, whether it's going to work, watching an advert or eating the evening meal. Given the massive influence of the private sector on happiness, wellbeing is a logical metric for business impact. In the future, we can expect many more businesses to measure their effects on happiness. If this sounds far-fetched, consider that just 20 years ago, few companies could report on their carbon footprint. Today, nearly 2,000 don't just measure it, but actively submit data to a scheme run by the transparency organization CDP.[15] Similar schemes for water, human rights and tax transparency are gathering speed.

A Wellthy Company measures and publishes a wellbeing footprint. As the emotional economy gathers speed, we might imagine some creative innovations. Employees could choose to work with organizations where wellbeing is highest. Non-governmental organizations (NGOs) could track how businesses create joy, misery, frustration and hope. Governments could regulate firms that cause the most damage to our emotions. And socially responsible investors could create funds that invest in firms with the best imprint on happiness.

The ultimate goal

To some, all this might sound like a trendy fad. Given the rousing interest, will happiness be forgotten when the next big idea comes along? The main reason to think this won't be the case is because wellbeing is no passing quirk. It has ancient roots. It's just that most organizations have lost sight of its relevance in the last 2,000 years.

The history of happiness reveals why wellbeing really is the only logical purpose – the *raison d'être* – for any socially minded organization. Aristotle is perhaps the most famous philosophical influence. He described wellbeing as the *summum bonum* – the "chief good". His explanation for the primacy of wellbeing illustrates its importance to every person and organization: "happiness, more than anything, is absolutely final. For we always choose it for the sake of itself and never for the sake of something else."[16] By this, he meant that we want to be happy for its own sake, not because it leads to anything else. All other things – money, peace, freedom, status – are means to that end. A rounded and satisfied life is a self-evident goal for everyone – individuals, society, governments and companies.

In the medieval period, the Italian friar St Thomas Aquinas picked up the same theme. He described how happiness was our true "last end" and the real goal of any rational being. So, a happy life can be thought of as an aspiration that unites us all. Then along came Jeremy Bentham, the philosopher, with his Eureka moment in the coffee shop. Inspired by David Hume and others, Bentham led the charge in articulating how happiness maximization was the greatest good for society. Other great thinkers such as John Stuart Mill further developed his ideas, adding that there are different types of happiness: quality matters too.[17]

The importance of wellbeing is by no means solely a Western concept. Confucianism and Taoism taught to focus on happiness for the self and others. Buddhism outlines a mindful path to wellbeing inspired by the *Happiness Verses* of Buddha's Dhammapada. Abu Hamid al-Ghazali, the Muslim scholar, wrote *The Alchemy of Happiness* in the early twelfth century.

So, the idea of happiness as our ultimate aim is ancient and universal. It is globally relevant to all cultures. It can apply just as much to private organizations as individuals and governments. What's new is the fact that we can accurately measure this goal. That means we can identify how the actions of any organization enhance happiness or undermine it. For those working in companies today, if wellbeing once seemed like a woolly idea, it's time for a rethink. Governments are measuring it. Employees benefit from it. Consumers are yearning for it. Which all begs the question: what can companies do about it?

A blueprint for action

This book sets out how any organization can source, manufacture and sell products and services that make everyone's lives more fulfilling. A Wellthy Company delivers a double dividend: growing human happiness and, in the process, creating profits. This wealth is shared with shareholders and society – through wages, taxes, dividends and reinvestment for growth.

I use the terms happiness, wellbeing, life satisfaction and quality of life throughout this book. There are all sorts of emotions and degrees of enjoying life. The smile induced from sipping a cup of tea is very different from the long-term satisfaction that the tea leaf plucker gets from a stable job. In general, this book is less about passing moods and more about how business can create longer-term, deeper feelings of a worthwhile existence.

Most happiness measures are subjective, meaning that they rely on individuals telling researchers about how they feel. Does this make the concepts too vague and unsuitable for business? Far from it. Just like market research, the measures are rigorous in aggregate. The data give a powerful insight into what elates and inspires, as well as worries and demotivates, across the world. We begin by examining the different types and measures of happiness in the next chapter.

The relationships between economic growth, wages and wellbeing are explored in Chapter 3. We'll see how more money and higher salaries rarely make for happier populations. The structure of the book then takes us on a journey across the wellbeing footprint of the business. We'll begin our travels at the top of the value chain in Chapter 4 and visit the farms and sweatshops of Africa and Asia to see how companies such as Apple and Mondelez are sourcing materials, parts and products that create contentment and sometimes misery. Then we'll examine workplaces in Chapter 5, discovering how the Wellbeing Purpose takes us beyond job satisfaction to raise staff's life satisfaction. The benefits include radically lower absence and staff turnover, and dramatically higher productivity and profit margins.

The impact of marketing will be unpicked in Chapter 6, where we'll ask some tough questions such as: does the McDonald's Happy Meal make kids happy? Examples from Nintendo, Pepsi and Unilever will illustrate how firms have juggled the tension between short-term hedonism and long-term satisfaction by building brands for wellbeing.

The Wellbeing Purpose is also about creating trust and social capital as a route to wellbeing and wealth creation. In Chapter 7, case studies from the Royal Bank of Scotland (RBS) and Johnson & Johnson (J&J) reveal how ethical behaviours and social investment affect community happiness. Finally, a new social purpose for business is outlined: raising life satisfaction for all. Drawing on examples from historic partnerships such as the UK's John Lewis and new start-ups such as Zappos, this final chapter sets out a game plan for commercial success based on a business model that maximizes human flourishing.

The CSR merry-go-round

Big business is facing a confluence of urgent challenges in the twenty-first century. The economic environment is intensely competitive. New regulatory threats can appear overnight. Cynical consumers have lost trust in companies, fuelled by tales of banks rigging exchange rates, carmakers fixing emissions tests, tech companies playing fast and loose with our data, energy and mining companies trashing pristine natural environments, and pharmaceutical firms denying life-saving drugs to the poorest.

Then there is the stench of scandals along the big brands' supply chains. We keep hearing stories of exhausted sweatshop labourers and aggressive deforestation in the developing world. And above it all, there is the chorus of protest at the perceived unfairness of corporate tax dodging and sky-high executive pay.

The digital revolution has allowed brands (and politicians) to interact with billions at a click. But social media is also creating the potential for unprecedented levels of scrutiny. Soon, every supplier and consumer in the world will have a smartphone, an opinion and a potentially awesome audience. The challenges and risks are mounting. So far, the record of big business in responding has, at best, been mixed. At its worst, it's been confused, ill-judged and self-damaging.

Partly in response to these pressures, the last 20 years have seen an explosion in the number of companies talking about corporate social responsibility (CSR) and sustainability. A mind-boggling 10,000 reports are now published by corporates every year on their CSR activities.[18] If you click on the website of any large multinational, you'll find a bewildering array of pledges and programmes. They cover things such as greenhouse gas emissions, protecting human rights, water use calculations, educational investments, biodiversity initiatives, health and safety, waste reduction – the list goes on and on.

The truth is that all of these initiatives have become something of a giant merry-go-round. They are a dizzy, noisy blur – a colourful carousel of pet projects that pull in different directions. Glistening community partnerships are the crowning jewel of the merry-go-round, a jolly dance between corporates and civil society that seek "impact." Despite impressive budgets, these initiatives typically fail to define what "impact" they seek to have, let alone measure it effectively.

As long as the CSR merry-go-round keeps spinning, the display looks impressive. It holds together. But the truth is that there is a gaping hole at the heart of the CSR carousel. There is no shared view about what responsible and sustainable business is trying to achieve. There is no consensus over what the *change* is that we aspire to create.

A sustainable future means nothing unless we agree what it is about life that we are trying to improve. We are all guilty of dancing around the central issue, dodging the question about what aspiration we have for companies in our world.

Do companies make life better?

The gaping hole at the heart of the CSR funfair comes down to a straightforward but unanswered question: do companies make life better? For the critics of capitalism, the answer is "no." They point to the injustice and indignity of many workplaces and a business model that fuels reckless consumption while trashing the planet for future generations. Whereas for those in the business community, the unspoken assumption is "yes." The production and exchange of goods only makes sense if we assume that those involved benefit from it.[19] Isn't it time that we worked out whether life is made better because of business? Then we could figure out how to boost quality of life most effectively through commerce and trade.

Let's be blunt about this. Issues such as unemployment, ill health and human rights abuses are each substantive topics in their own right. There are many tragic tales of human suffering at the hands of big business. But why do they matter? They matter because they result in unhappy people. Put more forcefully, a lack of a job, poor health and degrading working conditions are not *in of themselves* a problem. These issues deserve to be high on the agenda because they make millions of people utterly miserable.

Climate change does not matter in some abstract sense. It matters because the current effects on vulnerable communities, and future risk of catastrophe, present real barriers to leading a fulfilling life. The aim of responsible business should not be to invest in communities, protect the environment or provide decent jobs for their own sake. It should be to do all this because it helps people to get more out of life. Sustainable business should really be all about making life happier.

The causes and consequences of misery

The real problem with corporate social responsibility is that it almost always involves minimizing a negative. An environmental strategy reduces the destruction of the biosphere. A human rights policy seeks to protect against abuses. Few companies have grasped that responsible business should really be about making life better.

Of course, a business improving working conditions or the environment may, quite incidentally, address some of the *causes* of human suffering. But it's a roundabout route to happiness. Why not spell out the real ambition?

The Wellbeing Purpose addresses the *consequences* of commerce. Policies, programmes and products are designed to increase wellbeing and reduce misery.

Each of the choices made by a Wellthy Company contribute to the central purpose of boosting life satisfaction.

This might sound quite academic. But the distinction between tackling the *causes* or *consequences* of unhappiness is vital. It matters because some actions – such as paying people more and more money – have unclear or weak impacts on wellbeing, whereas others – such as a secure job and fulfilling work – typically result in major improvements.

Focusing on the wrong goal can be a waste of time and effort. Take the example of poverty. The United Nations has set a Global Goal of "zero poverty" by 2030. All businesses are being asked to play their part in achieving this. But it's a technical measure of income levels.[20] If the money doesn't come from jobs that are decent and worthwhile, hundreds of millions will still live in misery. What matters for wellbeing is relationships, health and meaningful work – not just having a certain wage level. By agreeing that happiness is the right end goal for everyone, we can tease out the best actions for companies to take. We can guide the investments to create a truly sustainable future that has people and their feelings at its heart.

A new corporate purpose

What is the social value of business? Some say it's all down to the economics. Companies produce goods and services that we want to buy. We purchase things that we expect to derive some benefit from. We work in places where the pay makes up for what we are asked to do.

Economists call this utility. But why do economic things matter? They don't matter in of themselves. They matter in as far as they make people happier.[21] Financial objectives and CSR ambitions such as poverty or climate change cannot be our end goal. Business's social, environmental and economic value *only* matters if it improves life.

It used to be said that shareholder returns were the aim of business, pure and simple. Today, for increasing numbers of companies, financial profitability is a by-product of success – not the main objective. In the years I've worked with companies on these issues, I've only once met a CEO who claimed that his main aim was to increase shareholder returns (an energy company, whose share price subsequently tanked with the oil price).

Instead, most business leaders get out of bed in the morning to do something for the world. Many chief executives speak of ambitions for game-changing solutions to global challenges. Some companies have begun to paint a picture of a purpose beyond profit. A social purpose explains *why* a company exists. It provides some meaning. But what should a business aspire to exist for?

The premise of this book is that there is no better purpose for business than to maximize society's wellbeing. As Jeremy Bentham discovered in a coffee shop over

250 years ago, the "greatest happiness of the greatest number" is a logical end that we can all agree on.

The Wellbeing Purpose is not about the scattergun approach of CSR. Activities aren't undertaken in the vague hope of "social impact." Instead, we start with defining the future we want to create for humanity: an economy of organizations that advance quality of life.

The social purpose of every organization should be to enable more lives to flourish. This can create wellbeing and wealth, through a more resilient, fast-growing and profitable firm. Companies can no longer afford to be silent on the overall objective of life on this planet. To understand the phenomenal potential, we must start with the science and ask: what makes us happy?

Notes

1 Aristotle, *Nicomachean Ethics*, Book I.
2 There is some debate over whether Bentham's original source was Priestley. However, Bentham was convinced that it was. See Bentham, J. (1834) Deontology, or the science of morality. *The British Critic, Quarterly Theological Review, and Ecclesiastical Record*, 16(32), October; and Crimmins, J. E. (2011). *Utilitarian Philosophy and Politics: Bentham's Later Years*. London: Bloomsbury.
3 The expression "wellbeing creation" in contrast to "wealth creation" has been used by Professor Lord (Richard) Layard to describe a new role for the state. See *Relationships and Good Health the Key to Happiness, Not Income*. Retrieved 26 February 2018, from www.lse.ac.uk/website-archive/newsAndMedia/news/archives/2016/12/Relationships-and-happiness.aspx.
4 A Google Scholar search for "wellbeing" OR "well-being" in the title of books, articles and other publications since 1986 yields 33,400 hits, excluding citations (calculated January 2016).
5 *Robert F. Kennedy Speeches*. Remarks at the University of Kansas (18 March 1968). John F. Kennedy Presidential Library and Museum.
6 Givel, M. (2015). Mahayana Buddhism and gross national happiness in Bhutan. *International Journal of Wellbeing*, 5(2), 14–27.
7 David Cameron's speech to Google Zeitgeist Europe (2006). *The Guardian*, 22 May.
8 Layard, R. (2011). *Happiness: Lessons from a New Science*. London: Penguin.
9 Brown, D. W. (2012). *The Real Change-Makers: Why Government is Not the Problem or the Solution*. Santa Barbara, CA: Praeger.
10 Hilton, A. (2015). The key question – is stagnation here to stay? *London Evening Standard*, 19 February.
11 Helliwell, J. F., Layard, R. & Sachs, J. (eds.) (2015). *World Happiness Report 2015*. New York: Sustainable Development Solutions Network.
12 Gallup (2012). *State of the American Workplace: Employee Engagement Insights for U.S. Business Leaders*. Washington, DC: Gallup.
13 Edelman (2018). *Trust Barometer*. New York: Edelman. US figures for trust in business were down 10 percentage points in 2018 versus 2017.
14 Forbes (2017). *Global 2000*. New York: Forbes Media.

15 CDP (2014). *Revealed: The Companies Doing the Most to Combat Climate Change*. Press release, 15 October. London: CDP.
16 Aristotle, *Nicomachean Ethics*, Book I, Chapter 4.
17 Mill, J. S. (1901). *Utilitarianism*. London: Longmans, Green & Company.
18 Corporate Citizenship (2015). *The Future of Reporting: From Routine to Strategic*. London: Corporate Citizenship.
19 Csikszentmihalyi, M. (2003). *Good Business: Leadership, Flow, and the Making of Meaning*. New York: Viking Penguin.
20 The indicator for this Sustainable Development Goal at the time of writing is the percentage of a population below $1.25 per day.
21 Oswald, A. J. (1997). Happiness and economic performance. *The Economic Journal*, *107*(445), 1815–1831.

Chapter 2

Science
Measuring the good life

> When you can measure what you are speaking about, and express it in numbers, you know something about it.
>
> Lord Kelvin, mathematician and physicist (1824–1907)[1]

Back in 2002, a monk was selected for an extraordinary experiment. Owing to a passion for meditation, Matthieu Ricard volunteered to be strapped into a magnetic resonance imaging (MRI) scanner. Dr Richard Davidson, a neuroscientist specializing in how the brain responds to emotions, attached nearly 250 sensors to his skull.

Since leaving a life in Paris and emigrating to the Himalayan foothills of India, Ricard had spent tens of thousands of hours in silent contemplation. Dr Davidson's purpose was to try to find out whether the monk's emotions could be quantified in the lab. Would they show up as any different from yours and mine?

Slipping calmly into the scanner, the monk was asked to lie still and ponder "unconditional love and compassion." As he settled into a deep, meditative trance, Dr Davidson couldn't quite believe what he saw. A surge of electromagnetic gamma waves flashed up on the screen. They were concentrated around the prefrontal cortex, the part of the brain associated with happiness, joy and enthusiasm.

The monk's readings for positive emotion were unlike anything that had been recorded in the science literature before. In the words of Dr Davidson, Ricard's brainwave readings were "off the chart."[2] When the results were published, Matthieu Ricard quickly became known as "the world's happiest man."[3]

Dr Davidson is director of the Laboratory for Affective Neuroscience at the University of Wisconsin–Madison. He has been strapping monks into brain scanners ever since he first noticed unusual readings from those who regularly meditate. What these experiments show is that emotions – just like physical pain – can be measured. Happiness can be traced on a computer screen, quantified in numbers. Wellbeing can be objectively calculated as it displays a physical reaction in the body.

But happiness, by its very nature, is something that we feel. It is an expression of our moods and experiences. Can we really measure something so subjective and unique to each person? Even if we can, what does a score such as 6.5 out of 10 really mean? Can business even do anything about this fantastical-sounding science?

The study of happiness has advanced at breakneck speed over the last 40 years. There is now a vast bank of research that reveals what shapes positive and negative emotions as well as feelings of a satisfied life. The findings have been tested and tested again. Various methodologies have been compared; different cultures have been analysed. The findings from these studies are quite consistent: there is a rigorous science to happiness.

This rich data set can help us to understand how the actions of commerce – from paying wages to developing life-changing products – assist and hinder how we feel about life. The conclusions have profound implications that can help companies to manage costs, reduce risks and grow revenues. But unlike Dr Davidson's experiments, most wellbeing is not measured by brain scans. Happiness is an intensely private, personal sentiment. It's usually calculated by a much more straightforward method: we ask people how they are feeling.

Now bear with me. To some readers, this might sound wishy-washy. The very idea of measuring how we feel may conjure up images of a hippy camp in the 1960s or a sci-fi movie from the 1980s. Business functions on facts. Managers can only make good decisions if there are reliable data. Of course, all business decisions require some judgement. You innovate a product or launch in a new market with estimates as well as a little intuition. Is the research on wellbeing rigorous enough to make decisions on procurement strategies, employee bonuses, the R&D pipeline and marketing plans? I want to show you in this chapter why it's not just good enough – it's so clear and compelling that any organization would be crazy to ignore the findings.

The meaning of wellbeing

The science of wellbeing is based on thousands of surveys of millions of people. We know what makes the average person happier, and which actions and situations are most likely to create misery. This means that business can do something to change perceptions of life. Before we discover what the latest research reveals, forgive me if I ask you a personal question. All things considered, how satisfied are you with your life as a whole these days?

Think seriously about this question for a moment. If I knocked on your door and posed that question, how would you respond after being told that 1 means you are "completely dissatisfied" and 10 means "completely satisfied"? Where would you put your satisfaction with your life *as a whole*? This question, or a variant of it, has been asked in nearly 100 countries countless times over the last 20 years.

Those who have answered it are statistically representative of almost 90% of the world's 7.5 billion people.[4]

When you think about how to reply, you are doing two things. First, there is a gut reaction guided by your current mood. Hopefully, you are feeling quite relaxed and stimulated while reading, or perhaps frustrated that I asked the question, or even impatient to get to the "what makes us happy" bit. That's coming. But if you thought about your answer for longer than half a second, then you probably also stepped back. By this, I mean that alongside your current emotional state, you also thought about your life in the round. The expression "life as a whole" – typically repeated twice by the questioner – is designed to prompt you to reflect on your satisfaction *in general terms*. Beyond the passing smile or agitation, how do you feel about life overall?

Defining wellbeing

Wellbeing is the degree to which an individual judges the overall quality of their life. On balance, how positive an appreciation does the farmer, factory worker or shopper have of their existence? This is measuring a perception. The question asks us to evaluate *our* life according to how *we* see things.

Academics use the term "subjective wellbeing." I use the expressions wellbeing, happiness, quality of life and life satisfaction throughout this book. Although they all have slightly different technical definitions, we are primarily interested in how individuals assess their lives in the round.

Drilling down a bit, wellbeing is made up of three parts: positive emotions and moods (such as joy, amusement and contentment); negative feelings (such as anxiety, anger and pain); and life satisfaction. Business affects all three areas. But the third part, life satisfaction, is the most substantive. It is the step back, the viewing of things overall, the personal evaluation.

When you made the assessment for yourself, you were estimating a gap. How wide is the difference between your life as you currently experience it and what you aspire to or imagine a good life to be?[5] When we examine whether companies make us more or less happy, I don't just mean whether a call centre infuriates or munching on a favourite chocolate bar creates a warm feeling. We are asking whether business raises contentment in the long run. Is the average person whose life is affected by companies making and selling their wares more satisfied overall as a result of their interactions?

Wellbeing is partly emotional (about how we experience positive and negative emotions) but also reflective (about standing back and evaluating life). Both the emotional (called "affective" by scientists) and life assessment ("cognitive") aspects are profoundly affected by our work environments,[6] as well as advertising, shopping, and using and experiencing all the products and services that companies create.

A worthwhile life

You may well be wondering: can it really be that simple? Does happiness boil down to jolly moods mixed with not too big a gap between the humdrum reality of life and our dreams for something better? Some experts have proposed a fourth element with an intriguing ethical dimension. They say that emotions and satisfaction are not enough. Instead, in order to be truly happy, we each need a sense of *meaning* that makes living worthwhile.[7]

Aristotle called this *eudaemonia*, which loosely translates as "human flourishing." He taught that the good life requires wisdom, virtue and strength of character. More recently, the positive psychology guru Martin Seligman has argued that everyone needs a sense of purpose and achievement for life to flourish.[8] This fourth dimension of wellbeing suggests that it's not enough to simply create warm feelings and overall contentment. Instead, businesses need to think more deeply about how meaning is created. The first step is providing good-quality work opportunities that enable a sense that life has a purpose. People want to work where they feel that both they and the organization are contributing to something greater. What role does the firm serve in society at large?

A social purpose explains *why* a business exists. It can act as a guiding light to take action in the supply chain, local community and even R&D department. We'll return to this crucial theme throughout this book and see how the Wellbeing Purpose can create meaning for all those whose lives are improved by the business.

Let's summarize what all this science has taught us so far. Happiness is made up of two in-the-moment feelings: positive and negative emotions. It is also rooted in longer-term, deeper evaluations of our life in the round. But we can't be truly happy without a feeling of worth and meaning, according to the fourth element.

When proponents of wellbeing say that we want more people to be happy, we are not talking about a zombie-like state of permanently grinning goons. A Wellthy Company aspires for more individuals to experience laughter and joy on a daily basis, and feel that life meets their hopes and feels worthwhile. We want fewer people, whether the farmer in the developing world or the status-seeking shopper in Manhattan, to feel angry, upset, depressed or that their existence lacks any meaning.

The massive effect of corporates on all these aspects has been overlooked for too long. But if that's the theory, is it really possible to measure it? Without reliable metrics, wellbeing cannot be studied, tracked and improved. Accurate measurement allows us to compare the happiness of very different individuals across the business footprint – and make the best choices to boost both wealth and wellbeing.

Measuring happiness

There are two main methods to measuring wellbeing: one calculates immediate emotions, and the second assesses life satisfaction. Emotional reports ask questions such as, "Did you laugh or smile yesterday?" or whether any anger or anxiety has been experienced. People find these pretty easy to answer. The results paint a vivid picture of day-to-day sentiments.

Gallup regularly asks adults in 143 countries about the positive experiences they had yesterday. More than 70% say that they felt a lot of enjoyment, smiled or laughed a lot, felt well-rested and felt treated with respect.[9] Despite the daily stories in the news of disaster and distress, most people around the world will have many happy feelings today. But that still leaves a large number of people who don't share in the joy. Three in 10 people experience a lot of worry or stress each day.[10] Gallup found that the negative scores are most prevalent in countries such as Iraq, Iran and Cambodia, and least common in China, Russia and Rwanda. Countries such as the UK and US fall somewhere in between. All this means that among the staff or customers of the average business anywhere in the world, around a third are likely to feel anxious or stressed on any given day.

Our moods can also be traced across the day, giving us an hour-by-hour account of which activities frustrate or motivate the most.[11] One study of 1,000 working women in America found that most unhappiness was experienced during the commute and at work – both activities related to their jobs. Most enjoyment came from socializing, relaxing, eating, exercising, praying or meditating, and being intimate with partners. Work is not the highlight of most people's schedule. Being with others brings most happiness. And guess which activity caused the lowest scores of all? Spending time with the boss.[12]

Life evaluations are measured differently. In order to quantify that stepping back – the perspective in the round – a simple scale is used. The question we asked earlier is one example from the World Values Survey. The General Social Survey has been asking Americans since 1972: "Taken all together, how would you say things are these days? Would you say that you are very happy, pretty happy, or not too happy?" These questions are designed to prompt a personal evaluation of how things are overall. About a third of Americans say that they are "very happy," 55% say they are "pretty happy," and one in nine say they are "not too happy." These figures have been remarkably constant over time. In the next chapter, we will explore why – despite rapidly rising incomes – happiness has not risen commensurately.

Gallup uses a similar rising scale where "the top of the ladder represents the best possible life for you and the bottom of the ladder represents the worst possible life for you." Notice the use of "for you" here. The researchers are not asking people to compare themselves to celebrities they've seen on TV or the life of their wildest dreams. The point of comparison is our own potential. We benchmark against colleagues and neighbours. The intention is to tease out that gap between daily reality and individual aspiration. This allows us to compare numbers between very different people. But we mustn't forget that these scores are all relative. A 10 out of 10 does not mean the same thing to a poor cotton farmer as a wealthy clothes shopper. Each will score their life according to very personal, very local criteria. Everyone is unique, and their dreams of what a good life looks like vary quite considerably.

Of course, norms change with economic and social development. As living standards rise, so do aspirations. Companies play a part in this when they open up timber-rich rainforests with new roads, strike oil in isolated communities or float balloons with internet access over remote areas. Bringing medicines or mobile phones to new markets changes perceptions of what a good life might look and feel like. In Chapter 6, we'll look at whether the critics of capitalism are justified in their charge that mass commerce ruins, rather than raises, life satisfaction.

The important point to reiterate is that all these measures are subjective. That's quite different from much of what we read about when it comes to development and CSR. Most companies use objective measures. Access to safe drinking water might get a tick in the box marked "quality of life." Poverty lines are drawn at a level relative to average earnings. But who decides that these issues matter? Who determines the cut-off?

Instead of predetermined criteria decided by academics and development agencies, the science of happiness starts with asking people how they feel. Statisticians then look for correlations between wellbeing and other measures, such as how much money we earn or whether we eat chocolate every day or work in a shoe factory. This allows us to work out whether having a Lamborghini and a $1 million bonus makes us happiest, or spending time with friends and family, owning a new mobile phone, working in certain industries or whatever.

The personal, subjective nature of wellbeing can be quite challenging. When it comes to global poverty, critics argue that it can make us too hasty to defend deprivation.[13] Just because the poor say they are happy, it doesn't mean that governments, companies and campaigners don't need to change things. The following chapters contain some case studies with astonishingly high levels of happiness reported among those living in financial poverty. They force us to question what deprivation really means and reconsider the role of business in development. But we mustn't forget that companies also have a role to play in raising the bar, championing perceptions of what makes for a really worthwhile life, rather than just accepting the status quo.

Although the questions are subjective, most people find them incredibly easy to answer. Refusals and "don't knows" are typically less than 1% – that's far better results than pollsters get from asking people about their household income.[14] People the world over seem to have a pretty solid grasp of what a good life feels like. Where illiteracy is widespread, pictures are used to illustrate the concepts. The questions have been translated and the answers tested in many different languages.

The results suggest that there is consistency around the world in understanding the concept of happiness. What matters for wellbeing is similar across cultures – as we will see in a moment. But individual scores vary wildly.

The geography of happiness paints a revealing picture of joy and misery that multinationals should be particularly cognizant of. In national rankings, countries such as Denmark, Switzerland and Norway usually come top. A collection of Sub-Saharan African nations alongside war-torn states such as Syria and Afghanistan typically rank bottom. Although the averages mask a few positive Syrians and some miserable Danes, the difference between the typical residents is shocking. The average score in Denmark is 7.5 on the life ladder; the typical resident of Togo or Burundi rates their life less than 3 out of 10.[15] So, far from being universally consistent, there are dramatic differences in the scores that people give to their lives.

The global diversity of happiness raises some fascinating questions when it comes to our purpose to maximize life satisfaction. For example, how much extra happiness might be created if you built that new factory in Burundi rather than Denmark? What about buying those peanuts from Togo rather than American farmers in Georgia? Strategies for optimizing the wellbeing footprint in developing countries are outlined in Chapter 4.

Robustness and reliability

The sum of all this science is a mind-boggling amount of data. Three reasons indicate that the findings are rigorous enough for companies to rely on them for decision-making. First, a vast number of studies with different methodologies in multiple cultures asking variants of the same questions to millions of people have all reached similar conclusions. This empirical data set, taken together, tells a forceful story about what does and does not make us happy.

Second, asking friends and family how happy they think someone *else* is backs up the self-reported scores.[16] This should give us confidence that subjective assessments are a pretty good reflection of how people really feel themselves.

Finally, the findings have been supported by objective measures such as monitoring stress hormones in the body and looking at the brain scans of meditating monks.[17] The physical science in the lab turns out to be consistent with the score from the researcher in the field. For all the criticisms of wellbeing, the idea that we can't measure it and don't know what makes people happy is simply not true.

One of the things that makes this book different is that it's based on science. Forget warm stories based on wishful thinking – the Wellbeing Purpose is founded on knowledge about the real influences of business on life. How do jobs and salaries affect how we feel? What about shopping habits? Even the links between what possessions we own and how we feel about life have been worked out.

Just as companies measure return on investment, product sales and customer satisfaction, a Wellthy Company also calculates a wellbeing footprint. In the final chapter, we'll explore the practical steps to developing a business model for life satisfaction. Rather than relying on guesswork, this empirical revolution has revealed what is most likely to make employees, suppliers, customers and communities happier. So, what does the science show?

What makes us happy?

Grumpy old men. Midlife crises. Carefree youngsters. Is there any truth to the stereotypes about happiness through different life stages? There is, it turns out – except the bit about grumpy old men. That's only partially true.

A huge number of studies have explored how wellbeing varies by gender, age and marital status. We'll start with these as they are the most comprehensive. Clearly, each individual that comes into contact with a company is different. Our genes, which shape our personality, play a surprisingly large part in making one person quite optimistic in outlook and another more negative. Nevertheless, when we add all the surveys up, we find that men and women are roughly equally happy. But women experience more of the highest and lowest levels of wellbeing.[18]

Satisfaction with life declines across all cultures from the dizzying heights of the teenage years to lower levels in the early thirties and midlife.[19] So, younger employees are generally likely to be more satisfied with life, and older hands less so. But the fall is not particularly steep, and wellbeing increases again as people get older. Why? Because we finish work and retire. Some grumpiness returns towards the end of life as the trials of old age kick in.[20] But let's be honest: the data yet again paint a depressing picture for business. The highest levels of happiness occur before entering the workforce and only shoot up again after quitting it.

Marriage can help. Another consistent finding is that those who are married or in a stable relationship are, on average, much happier than the single, separated, divorced or widowed. But this illustrates an age-old problem in science. Does getting married cause wellbeing to increase? Or are positive people more likely to wed? The same issue crops up with exercise – something that many food, drink and sports brands are keen to promote. Regular exertion correlates with happiness. But does all that sweating stimulate the positive feelings? Or are miserable people just less likely to exercise?

One study of Dutch teenagers discovered that those who regularly exercised had better moods and higher wellbeing. However, they then looked at twins. When one twin exercised and another didn't, the difference in happiness disappeared. This suggests that some underlying cause – inherited from parents – could cause the genetically optimistic to get out and exercise more.[21] So, we need to be careful. Just because something correlates with happiness, it doesn't mean it causes it.

A second complication is that it's never just one thing that determines how we feel about life. If you think about it, happiness is not really a linear scale. When I asked you to consider your own satisfaction on the ladder from 0 to 10, you were actually balancing a whole host of different influences on your life. How is work going? Is your health good? What about relationships with family and friends?

To complicate things further, sometimes our feelings contradict one and other. When devouring a large box of chocolates, we might get a warm, satisfied feeling alongside pangs of guilt, or even worry if our doctor warned us to watch our waistline. When a challenging project keeps us late at work, we might feel a valued part of the team, but also exhausted, lonely and wishing we were elsewhere.

Scientists deal with this by looking at something called the different domains of life. The domains include our occupation, family, health, economic situation, friends, community and leisure time. Each domain interacts with the others, so a miserable time at work can affect how we feel about family and our health. Equally, it's perfectly possible for someone to be very content with their job and unhappy in the other domains, and so unhappy overall. This is why job satisfaction is quite separate from life satisfaction.[22] If a firm's impact on wellbeing was all about being happy at work, it would be a simpler matter to address.

Our purpose is much more ambitious. What interests us is how companies elevate (and diminish) wellbeing in the round. The impacts are felt in local communities, shopping malls and homes, through advertising on our screens and the brands we use. Companies affect our health as well as our economic situation. Some shape family life, friendships and leisure time through their work practices and product portfolios. Job satisfaction is a small part of a much bigger story.

A perspective on time

Another consideration is timescales. That box of chocolates illustrates this perfectly. The short-term joy of eating a treat can become bad for your health, and so wellbeing, if you binge to excess every day. An unaffordable shopping trip on a credit card might create fleeting joy for a few days but perpetuate debt misery for years more.

When a brand claims that it makes us happy – as Coca-Cola's famous strapline "Open Happiness" implied – there is a world of difference between immediate gratification and longer-term life satisfaction. The impact on life may be dramatically different depending on the time frame in question. Consider the anger spawned by some truly shocking customer service. It doesn't need to make us miserable for the whole week, less still unsatisfied with life overall. If it did, customers of many energy and airline firms (the ones that are always bottom of the customer league tables) would be thoroughly depressed. In fact, most people's lives are made a lot better thanks to reliable and affordable energy and cheap air travel. So, companies can have immediate effects on our emotions that are very different from their impacts on life satisfaction over a longer time frame.

All this means that we cannot really compare the happiness of a Singaporean shopper buying a mobile phone with that of an Indian farmer given life-saving access to clean drinking water, or the elation an employee gets from being told they've got a massive pay rise to the joy of eating a tasty chocolate bar. Each might tip a person's feelings from a "6" to an "8" when asked how happy they feel *at that moment*. But there is a vast difference between momentary elation and deeper, long-lasting satisfaction with life. The issue of timescales is particularly pertinent when it comes to marketing and products, something that we will examine in Chapter 6.

The comparison challenge hasn't stopped some fascinating calculations from being made. For example, the UK Government's Department for Culture, Media and Sport has estimated that regular dance classes or swimming lessons can boost your happiness by the equivalent of a £1,600 ($2,200) pay rise.[23] Going to the cinema once a week has been valued at an astonishing £9,000 ($12,600) a year.[24] Each of these activities is an entertaining experience that is typically shared with others. Dancing and swimming can improve fitness too. That's why they can be so great for wellbeing.

There is, however, a limit to what any organization – government or business – can actually influence. Some scholars have suggested that about half of our life satisfaction is determined by genetics. This could mean that life circumstances, and the influence of commerce, only marginally affect human happiness.[25] Others believe that our behaviours and experiences profoundly shape how we feel about life. After all, that's the premise of so many self-help books. If we can't influence how happy we feel, why bother trying? The truth lies somewhere in between. We shouldn't overemphasize the role of business. There are limits to what companies can achieve. But the science has identified three essential touchpoints where business can profoundly transform lives.

The three vital ingredients of wellbeing

There are three vital ingredients to the Wellbeing Purpose, three core components to life satisfaction that each and every company can affect. The first action is rudimentary but truly life-changing: a Wellthy Company creates jobs. Having employment provides a sense of meaning and value in life. Work provides social interaction, a structure to the day and a sense of usefulness and personal purpose.

Although happiness typically falls as we enter the workforce and rises with retirement, it's unemployment during working years that causes the most misery. Being out of work results in drops in wellbeing well beyond what we'd expect from a loss of income alone.[26] Study after study has shown that involuntary unemployment – people who want work but can't find it – is one of the biggest causes of misery our world has ever invented. The experience of being out of a job is so bad for happiness that it has a comparable affect to the death of a loved one.[27] Unemployment is the only major life event from which people do not fully recover within five years.[28]

The experience of unemployment doesn't just affect individuals – it makes entire communities unhappy. According to some estimates, the knock-on impacts are twice as great across whole localities as those felt by the individual who is out of work.[29]

A Wellthy Company aspires to create jobs, retain jobs and grow job opportunities across the value chain. Creating decent jobs, in the right places, is the single most important way that companies can improve life for billions on this planet. We'll return to this theme throughout the book.

Besides job creation, what else matters for wellbeing? The next two vital ingredients have an equally strong evidence base. Back in 1978, a young academic by the name of Reed Larson set out on a mission. He wanted to find a definitive answer to the question: what makes older Americans happy? He dived into the archives and explored over 30 years of research. This was at a time before computers and the internet made such tasks a simple matter of punching in some keywords.

Working out of the University of Chicago, Larson dug out journals stretching back to the 1940s when studies first began asking people about their satisfaction with life. His conclusions in 1978 – after reviewing three decades of studies – are still relevant today. One major factor jumped out as accounting for most of the variation in happiness: health. But he also identified another vital ingredient: how much social interaction people had, such as spending time with friends and neighbours.[30]

Forty years on, these two findings still ring true not just for retirees, but across the world for all of us. We literally now have a *lifetime* of research that backs this up: our physical and mental health, alongside personal connections, are the two most critical determinants of happiness.

Health and relationships are the two ingredients that every business influences through its employment practices, wider business operations, and the products and services it develops and sells. Some of these impacts are positive and do huge amounts to enhance life. But other influences are negative – a great untold story of how companies are often unexpectedly making people less satisfied with their lot.

Physical and mental health

Let's start with health. Those who rate their health as "very bad" typically score their life satisfaction a massive three points less (out of 10) compared to those in "very good" health.[31] This is for two reasons. First, healthier people are more likely to feel positive about life. The experience is more enjoyable and optimism is boosted. Second, happier people are less likely to fall ill as a positive outlook instils a certain resilience to some health issues.

A few health conditions have a particularly harsh impact on wellbeing. Heart disease and strokes – both rising due to poor diets and lifestyles – are particularly dramatic causes of unhappiness.[32] The effect of diabetes is similar to losing a large income, perhaps as much as a 60% pay cut.[33] When it comes to long-term disabilities, the evidence is somewhat surprising. Adaptation plays a crucial role in mitigating unhappiness. Studies show that those living with long-term illnesses typically become accustomed to the changes remarkably quickly.[34]

Of all the health impediments, psychological illness is the most damaging. Mental health has a huge impact on wellbeing. According to the latest research, more people are in misery due to mental illness than poverty, unemployment or physical ill health.[35] Those who experience severe anxiety and depression have been estimated to feel the equivalent to a drop in income of £44,000 ($62,000) in the UK – well in excess of the average salary.[36] Good mental health has a powerful, positive effect on life satisfaction. Self-esteem, personal confidence and self-worth all contribute to feeling good about life.

In order to maximize wellbeing, companies need to boost, not reduce, physical and mental health. No business can claim to be making our world happier unless it is also making us healthier. In Chapters 5 and 6, we'll see how companies affect the health of staff and their customers.

Social relationships

The third vital ingredient is the strength of our relationships. The presence of a good network seems to matter more than any other external factor.[37] For young students, those who engage in the most social activity often report the very highest levels of wellbeing.[38] During periods of high stress, how much social support someone has is one of the biggest predictors of their overall happiness.[39]

Companies affect our personal connections at home, at work and through the services they sell. Work environments are a social setting that can be designed to stimulate interactions. Industries such as transport, entertainment, media and technology can bring customers closer together, or sometimes drive us further apart. In the digital world, where would modern relationships be without the mobile phone to stay in touch with loved ones?

Social media is the latest manifestation of how business is fostering ties between billions of people. From this standpoint, Facebook could be the world's most powerful force for happiness. But there is a well-documented downside to these digital connections. Too much time online increases unhappiness. Those excluded, as well as the addicts suffering from fear of missing out (FOMO), often report deep dissatisfaction. We will examine the lessons from businesses that have grown and destroyed social capital in Chapter 7, and Chapter 8 sets out a strategy to create experiential products that maximize happiness.

Traditional responsible business offers worryingly little when it comes to life satisfaction. In fact, some CSR and sustainability programmes are dressed up to hide the fact that companies are corroding life – a great community education programme from a tobacco company, for example. Many technology firms talk about transforming the world – but dig into their supply chains, and the story is one of poor health, insecure jobs and neglectful conditions.

Anything business does to cut jobs, weaken health and undermine relationships is destructive to wellbeing. In the future, we can expect more stakeholders – such as employees, regulators and even some investors – to view such firms as inherently damaging to life. Conversely, any action to create jobs, improve health and strengthen relationships is a step towards a strategy for maximizing wellbeing. These three vital ingredients are the backbone of the Wellbeing Purpose.

Autonomy, education and security

Four other factors have clear links to life satisfaction. They are worth exploring, albeit briefly, as many companies can have significant impacts on them. The first is personal autonomy, which means how much control and influence we feel we have over life. When we feel empowered to shape our own choices, wellbeing rises. The work environment can have an enormous effect on these feelings. We'll look at the specific actions a Wellthy Company takes to promote agency and autonomy in Chapter 5.

Second is training and education. For those who enjoy learning, it's tempting to assume that the more education one has, the happier we become. The truth is that there is mixed evidence on the benefits of education.[40] Some research in the UK found that those who'd completed at least a university degree had significantly *lower* levels of job satisfaction and higher mental distress (including lower confidence and less self-esteem). However, studies from Switzerland, the US and Latin America have reached the opposite conclusion: higher education has a positive relationship with life satisfaction.[41] This may be due to cultural differences in the value of learning, as well as the expectations that studying creates. With increased opportunities, our aspirations for life may rise beyond what we can attain. Don't forget, it's the gap between dreams and reality that determines life satisfaction.

Training and skills development are particularly relevant for companies. Here, the research is surprisingly limited. Some studies suggest what seems instinctive: providing more training increases satisfaction with jobs and life overall.[42] Research from China has found the opposite, possibly because increased opportunities for training are associated with more at-risk jobs.[43] The picture is far from clear when it comes to training, and there is no doubt more research to be done on this topic.

Third, personal safety and security are essential for wellbeing. If we don't feel safe, we can't feel happy. Most obviously, this means providing a safe working environment. There are clear links between wellbeing and an absence of violence.[44] As we'll see in Chapter 4, ensuring supply chains are free from cruelty and intimidation is a basic requirement for any multinational with a Wellbeing Purpose. Another highly significant factor is corruption. This has been systematically linked to wellbeing: more corruption means more misery[45] – something we will explore how companies affect in Chapter 7.

The environment

How safe and secure we feel is shaped by our environment. Levels of social unrest are aggravated by drought, water shortages, hurricanes and the migrations that follow such catastrophes. While many companies think about green initiatives as a promise to future generations, the evidence suggests that there is a more immediate impact on those living today. For example, extreme weather events – aggravated by human-induced climate change – are already having a detrimental impact on happiness in some communities.[46] Corporate leadership on climate change is significant for wellbeing because the effects are set to create even more instability and unhappiness.

Our local environment profoundly shapes how we feel about life. Green spaces can create a surprisingly sharp boost to positive feelings. Levels of air pollution show high correlations with happiness.[47] Even levels of greenhouse gas emissions have been linked to wellbeing.[48] In Chapter 4, we will see how environmentally sensitive supply chain management can have a direct influence on wellbeing for farmers and their communities. The important point is that responsible environmental management can deliver wellbeing benefits today.

The things that make life feel better seem to be quite consistent across the world. Good health matters just as much to the Madagascan vanilla bean farmer as the Californian ice cream consumer. Strong friendships are as important to the Shenzhen production line worker as the São Paulo shopkeeper.

But jobs vary hugely. The career we end up in has enormous implications for our happiness. In the UK, the occupations with the lowest scores for life satisfaction are coal miners, street cleaners, market traders, windscreen fitters and dry cleaners.[49] These are low-paid jobs. Near the top of the list are the chief executives – the highest paid. Perhaps it's simply a case of more money means more happiness?

A closer look at the data raises serious doubts. Sports players come top – some highly paid, but many so badly paid they are in effect amateurs. The clergy are second, and rank top in some US studies.[50] Religious leaders certainly witness life's highs and lows, but few could be described as well remunerated. Air traffic controllers come third on the UK list – a life-and-death job, often under high pressure.

Then there is an extraordinary range of low-paid jobs that score amazingly highly for life satisfaction: beauticians and butchers; car valets, childminders and counsellors; dental nurses; farmworkers, fishmongers, fitness instructors and florists; hairdressers and horticulturalists; pharmacy assistants, potters and post office clerks; secretaries and sports coaches; teaching assistants, textile makers and travel agents; upholsterers and undertakers; and weavers and waiters. Each receive a typical salary of less than £20,000 ($28,000) but score more than 7.6 out of 10 for life satisfaction – above average. Something curious is going on here. Can it be right that incomes don't really relate to wellbeing?

Notes

1 William Thomson Kelvin (1883). *Lecture to Institution of Civil Engineers*, London, 3 May.
2 Zetter, K. (2003). Scientists meditate on happiness. *Wired*, 16 September.
3 Bates, C. (2012). Is this the world's happiest man? *Daily Mail*, 31 October. Retrieved 13 August 2016, from www.dailymail.co.uk/health/article-2225634/Is-worlds-happiest-man-Brain-scans-reveal-French-monk-abnormally-large-capacity-joy-meditation.html.
4 *World Values Survey*. Retrieved 8 June 2018, from www.worldvaluessurvey.org/.
5 Pavot, W. & Diener, E. (2013). Happiness experienced: the science of subjective well-being. In S. A. David, I. Boniwell & A. C. Ayers (eds.), *The Oxford Handbook of Happiness* (pp. 134–151). Oxford: Oxford University Press.
6 Caza, B. & Wrzesniewski, A. (2013). How work shapes well-being. In S. A. David, I. Boniwell & A. C. Ayers (eds.), *The Oxford Handbook of Happiness* (pp. 693–710). Oxford: Oxford University Press.
7 Lyubomirsky, S. (2008). *The How of Happiness: A Scientific Approach to Getting the Life You Want*. New York: Penguin.
8 Seligman, M. E. (2012). *Flourish: A Visionary New Understanding of Happiness and Well-Being*. New York: Simon & Schuster.
9 Gallup (2015). *Mood of the World Upbeat on International Happiness Day*, 19 March. Retrieved 13 August 2016, from www.gallup.com/poll/182009/mood-world-upbeat-international-happiness-day.aspx.
10 Gallup (2015). *Global Emotions Report*. Washington, DC: Gallup.
11 Krueger, A. B., Kahneman, D., Schkade, D., Schwarz, N. & Stone, A. A. (2009). National time accounting: the currency of life. In A. B. Krueger (ed.), *Measuring the Subjective Well-Being of Nations: National Accounts of Time Use and Well-Being* (pp. 9–86). Chicago, IL: University of Chicago Press.
12 Kahneman, D., Krueger, A. B., Schkade, D. A., Schwarz, N. & Stone, A. A. (2004). A survey method for characterizing daily life experience: the day reconstruction method. *Science*, 306(5702), 1776–1780.
13 Sen, A. K. (1990). Development as capability expansion. In S. Fukuda-Parr et al. (eds.), *Readings in Human Development*. New Delhi & New York: Oxford University Press.
14 Kahneman, D. & Krueger, A. B. (2006). Developments in the measurement of subjective well-being. *Journal of Economic Perspectives*, 20(1), 3–24.

15 Helliwell, J. F., Layard, R. & Sachs, J. (eds.) (2015). *World Happiness Report 2015*. New York: Sustainable Development Solutions Network.

16 Sandvik, E., Diener, E. & Seidlitz, L. (1993). Subjective well-being: the convergence and stability of self-report and non-self-report measures. *Journal of Personality*, *61*(3), 317–342.

17 Diener, E. & Tov, W. (2012). National accounts of well-being. In K. C. Land, A. C. Michalos & M. J. Sirgy (eds.), *Handbook of Social Indicators and Quality-of-Life Research*. New York & London: Springer.

18 Fujita, F., Diener, E. & Sandvik, E. (1991). Gender differences in negative affect and well-being: the case for emotional intensity. *Journal of Personality and Social Psychology*, *61*(3), 427–434.

19 Helliwell, J. F., Layard, R. and Sachs, J. (eds.) (2015). *World Happiness Report 2015*. New York: Sustainable Development Solutions Network.

20 Pavot, W. & Diener, E. (2013). Happiness experienced: the science of subjective well-being. In S. A. David, I. Boniwell & A. C. Ayers (eds.), *The Oxford Handbook of Happiness* (pp. 134–151). Oxford: Oxford University Press.

21 Bartels, M., De Moor, M., Van der Aa, N., Boomsma, D. & De Geus, E. (2012). Regular exercise, subjective wellbeing, and internalizing problems in adolescence: causality or genetic pleiotropy? *Frontiers in Genetics*, *3*, 1–12.

22 Dockery, A. M. (2005). The happiness of young Australians: empirical evidence on the role of labour market experience. *Economic Record*, *81*(255), 322–335.

23 Fujiwara, D., Kudrna, L. & Dolan, P. (2014). *Quantifying and Valuing the Wellbeing Impacts of Culture and Sport*. London: Department for Culture, Media and Sport.

24 Marsh, K., MacKay, S., Morton, D., Parry, W., Bertranou, E., Lewsie, J., Sarmah, R. & Dolan, P. (2010) *Understanding the Value of Engagement in Culture and Sport*. London: Department for Culture, Media and Sport.

25 Lykken, D. & Tellegen, A. (1996). Happiness is a stochastic phenomenon. *Psychological Science*, *7*(3), 186–189.

26 Layard, R. (2011). *Happiness: Lessons from a New Science*. London: Penguin.

27 O'Donnell, G., Deaton, A., Durand, M., Halpern, D. & Layard, R. (2014). *Wellbeing and Policy*. London: Legatum Institute.

28 Clark, A. E., Diener, E., Georgellis, Y. & Lucas, R. E. (2008). Lags and leads in life satisfaction: a test of the baseline hypothesis. *The Economic Journal*, *118*(529), F222–F243.

29 Helliwell, J. F. & Huang, H. (2014). New measures of the costs of unemployment: evidence from the subjective well-being of 3.3 million Americans. *Economic Inquiry*, *52*(4), 1485–1502.

30 Larson, R. (1978). Thirty years of research on the subjective well-being of older Americans. *Journal of Gerontology*, *33*(1), 109–125. Larson also identified socio-economic and several other variables as significant.

31 Evans, J. (2011). *Findings from the National Well-Being Debate*. London: Office for National Statistics.

32 Dolan, P., Peasgood, T. & White, M. (2008). Do we really know what makes us happy? A review of the economic literature on the factors associated with subjective well-being. *Journal of Economic Psychology*, *29*(1), 94–122.

33 Ferrer-i-Carbonell, A. & Van Praag, B. (2002). The subjective costs of health losses due to chronic diseases: an alternative model for monetary appraisal. *Health Economics*, *11*(8), 709–722.

34   Dolan, P., Peasgood, T. & White, M. (2008). Do we really know what makes us happy? A review of the economic literature on the factors associated with subjective well-being. *Journal of Economic Psychology*, *29*(1), 94–122.

35   Clark, A.E., Flèche, S., Layard, R., Powdthavee, N. & Ward, G. (2018). *The Origins of Happiness*. Princeton, NJ: Princeton University Press.

36   Fujiwara, D. & Dolan, P. (2014). *Valuing Mental Health: How a Subjective Wellbeing Approach Can Show Just How Much It Matters*. London: UK Council for Psychotherapy.

37   O'Donnell, G., Deaton, A., Durand, M., Halpern, D. & Layard, R. (2014). *Wellbeing and Policy*. London: Legatum Institute.

38   Diener, E. & Seligman, M. E. (2002). Very happy people. *Psychological Science*, *13*(1), 81–84.

39   Achor, S. (2012). Positive intelligence. *Harvard Business Review*, *90*(1), 100–102.

40   Clark, A.E., Flèche, S., Layard, R., Powdthavee, N. & Ward, G. (2018). *The Origins of Happiness*. Princeton, NJ: Princeton University Press.

41   Powdthavee, N. (2010). *The Happiness Equation: The Surprising Economics of Our Most Valuable Asset*. London: Icon Books.

42   Felstead, A., Gallie, D., Green, F. & Inanc, H. (2013). *Skills at Work in Britain: First Findings from the Skills and Employment Survey 2012*. Cardiff: Cardiff University Press.

43   Appleton, S. & Song, L. (2008). Life satisfaction in urban China: components and determinants. *World Development*, *36*(11), 2325–2340.

44   Schimmel, J. (2009). Development as happiness: the subjective perception of happiness and UNDP's analysis of poverty, wealth and development. *Journal of Happiness Studies*, *10*(1), 93–111.

45   Helliwell, J. F. & Huang, H. (2008). How's your government? International evidence linking good government and well-being. *British Journal of Political Science*, *38*(4), 595–619.

46   Rehdanz, K. & Maddison, D. (2005). Climate and happiness. *Ecological Economics*, *52*(1), 111–125.

47   Welsch, H. (2002). Preferences over prosperity and pollution: environmental valuation based on happiness surveys. *Kyklos*, *55*(4), 473–494; Welsch, H. (2006). Environment and happiness: valuation of air pollution using life satisfaction data. *Ecological Economics*, *58*(4), 801–813.

48   Apergis, N. (2018). The impact of greenhouse gas emissions on personal well-being: evidence from a panel of 58 countries and aggregate and regional country samples. *Journal of Happiness Studies*, *19*(1), 69–80.

49   *Personal Wellbeing for Major and Sub-Major Standard Occupation Codes (SOC10)* (obtained from author's Freedom of Information Act request to the UK Cabinet Office, 2015).

50   Smith, T. W. (2007). Job satisfaction in the United States, cited in Powdthavee, N. (2010). *The Happiness Equation: The Surprising Economics of Our Most Valuable Asset*. London: Icon Books.

Chapter 3

Money
Wages and wellbeing

> Men do not desire to be rich, but to be richer than other men.
>
> John Stuart Mill (1806–1873)[1]

The odds of winning were 292 million to 1. But that didn't stop them coming. Americans were four times more likely to be struck by an asteroid than to win the largest lottery draw in history. By 13 January 2016, the Powerball jackpot had hit a staggering $1.5 billion. As dawn broke, long lines had formed outside stores across the country. Extra staff were drafted in to help sell the tickets. Men in suits waited alongside mothers with prams; people from all walks of life wanted to be in with a chance of winning. What would you do with such a life-changing amount?

The figure of $1.5 billion was so incomprehensibly large that billboards – built to show millions – had to be extended to cope with the extra digits. This was the largest lottery jackpot ever – it would be a life-changing amount for anyone lucky enough to scoop a share of the prize. But would it make the winners happy?

How happy would *you* be if you won the lottery? Every week, hundreds of millions of people around the world gamble their cash on a dream. There's clearly some fun in the luck of the draw. But many buy into a hope that a big payout will make life feel a lot happier.

Back in 1978, a team of researchers showed this to be an illusion. Philip Brickman, Dan Coates and Ronnie Janoff-Bulman interviewed 22 winners of the Illinois State Lottery, a third of whom had won $1 million (worth about $4 million in today's money). They found that winners were no more likely to be satisfied with life than a control group who had had no such "luck." Indeed, when asked to rate how happy they expected to be in a couple of years' time, their responses were no different from paralysed accident victims.[2] But if suddenly winning large sums of money doesn't make us happier, does a company giving you a higher salary or big bonus help?

Philosophers have spent millennia pondering the links between wealth and wellbeing. Most people *think* that more money will make them happier. When asked, individuals typically say that they'd need about 20% more income to be completely happy.[3] But the truth is far more interesting.

Companies pay salaries to employees, generate incomes in their supply chains and create products that we all need money to buy. We need to understand the links between money and happiness to maximize the private sector's impact on wellbeing. Given a choice between raising salaries or giving staff more time off work, which does most for quality of life? Does paying bigger wages and mega-bonuses to top employees create more satisfaction? Does ensuring a decent wage for the poorest, perhaps in a distant plantation at the top of the supply chain, affect how anyone feels about life? In short, what we need to know is: how *much* does money matter? To find the answers, we must go back nearly half a century to a landmark study that first teased out the fascinating relationship between wealth and wellbeing.

The Easterlin paradox

In 1970, a fellow at Stanford University named Richard Easterlin set out to unlock the mystery of how income relates to happiness. He dug out over 25 years' worth of data. He crunched the numbers from around 30 different surveys. He examined wellbeing in 19 different countries and compared the scores to detailed calculations on the economy. What he found was startling.

Easterlin worked out that within any country, the rich are always happier than the poor. However, when he compared statistics *between* nations, he found something quite different. Some wealthier countries had low levels of wellbeing while some poorer nations had surprisingly happy populations. But what really stirred things up was when he looked at the time series. Did rising incomes increase happiness as a society developed?

Piecing together data from 1946 to 1970 for the US, he tracked a sharply growing economy. But he found no clear increases in wellbeing during that time. In what is now known as the Easterlin paradox, he proposed that as countries get richer, we don't get any happier.[4] Similar findings have been shown for the UK: despite buying power more than doubling since the 1970s, average wellbeing has remained stubbornly flat.[5]

Since Richard Easterlin published his groundbreaking research, his findings have been supported by many others. Take two individuals at random, and the richer is likely to be happier than the poorer. But above a certain pay level, additional income doesn't make the poorer or richer any more satisfied *in the long run*.[6] This insight is profound, but it's by no means new. Jeremy Bentham, the philosopher we met in the Introduction, proposed an upper limit to the wealth–happiness relationship over 200 years ago:

Of two people having unequal fortunes, he who has most wealth must . . . be regarded as having most happiness. But the quantity of happiness will not go on increasing in anything near the same proportion as the quantity of wealth: ten thousand times the quantity of wealth will not bring with it ten thousand times the quantity of happiness.[7]

What does all this mean for companies? Although income and happiness are correlated, studies across the world show that the effects are modest and diminish over time.[8] This should cause some alarm. Our whole economic system is built on growth. Every day, hundreds of millions of businesses pay wages to employees and dividends to their owners. Each and every corporation is trying to grow. But beyond keeping up with inflation (which erodes relative living standards), the science suggests that there is no automatic link between more money and wellbeing. How can we explain this?

Explaining the money mystery

Imagine you are given a whopping 30% pay rise tomorrow. How would you feel? Would it make life any happier? For most people, there is a bounce in both satisfaction with the job and life overall. Now imagine that your salary stays the same but you find out that everyone else has got a 30% rise. This tends to make most people pretty irate. But looked at objectively, this reaction is irrational. Your buying power and living standards haven't changed one bit (assuming all that cash doesn't cause prices to go up in your area). You can still buy your daily espresso and rent a two-bedroom flat. It's just that you might see your colleagues slurping double grande lattes and moving into three-bedroom penthouses.

Our satisfaction with life depends on how we feel we are doing compared to others.[9] Happiness is affected by relative pay.[10] When the whole population's income is going up, it's impossible for everyone to get wealthier than average. The gains in the economy cancel out the gains in happiness in the long run. Once we reach a certain level of wealth, we can only get happier if we have more money *compared to everyone else*.

One study from Chile found that if the salaries of your peer group go up by 10%, you'll need a 25% raise to recover the same level of satisfaction with your job.[11] For any individual, this means it's typically better to be well paid relative to others in a low-paying organization rather than take a pay rise but be lower down the rung in a higher-paying firm.

We often compare ourselves to friends or neighbours. But more often than not, our reference group for wages is our colleagues.[12] Giving a pay rise to one employee could well make that individual happier – at least in the immediate term.

After all, relative to everyone else, they should feel higher up the pecking order. But giving the whole company a rise probably won't make any difference – unless staff compare themselves to neighbours and friends in less fortunate organizations.

These findings have significant implications for companies, particularly large ones that pay salaries to hundreds of thousands of employees. They suggest that across the board, pay rises and bonuses will do little to raise happiness. While there might be a short-term bounce of joy, the long-term effects on wellbeing are highly questionable.[13]

Alongside our relative rank, a second explanation for the tenuous link between pay and happiness is adaptation. When the context changes, we change our expectations. It's the reason why the lottery winners, over time, ended up no happier than anyone else, indeed no more satisfied than paralysed accident victims who had become accustomed to their tragic circumstances.

There is no automatic rise in wellbeing from increasing incomes because, collectively, our needs, wants, experiences and expectations change as money grows. The speed of adaptation to rising income can be surprisingly fast; any positive effects on happiness seem to completely wear off within a few years. For example, in China's rapidly growing cities, migrants at first succeed in getting higher incomes than their rural peers. But their aspirations adapt remarkably quickly to their new environment. Life satisfaction actually ends up lower.[14]

At the top of the hierarchy, adaptation explains why senior executives are no happier as a result of bumper pay packages. We've seen some lively debates in the media – and at shareholder meetings – about whether sky-high bonuses are merited. If some stakeholders are angry, the wellbeing research suggests it won't be making the CEOs any happier either.

For the richest in society, there really is no clear relationship between having oodles of wealth and happiness. The levels of life satisfaction among the super-wealthy in *Forbes* or the *Sunday Times Rich List* have been shown to be little different from the rest of the population.[15]

What, then, of those at the bottom of the pay scale? Surely money matters hugely to those farming food in the developing world, packaging goods in factories, moving them through docks and on to trucks, selling soda and sweets by the roadside, and then picking up the trash at the very end?

The trash pickers of Nicaragua

One of the dirtiest, most dangerous and worst-paid jobs in the world is picking waste in Nicaragua. The trash pickers in the city of León scour the tips for plastic, metal, glass and cardboard that is sold on for recycling. Half earn less than $40 for an entire month's labour – that's less than most Americans make in a few hours of work.

Their working conditions are stinking, unhealthy and unsafe. A huge stigma is attached to their work; these are life's true outcasts. At night, the trash pickers trudge back to overcrowded, makeshift shacks. In their slums, robbery and even murder are a daily reality. In short, this is one of the most oppressive jobs in the most unsavoury conditions in one of the poorest and most dangerous cities on earth. And it's all for very little pay. Can any of these workers possibly describe their lives as happy?

A Spanish researcher named José Juan Vázquez set out to find out. He tracked down all 99 garbage pickers in Nicaragua's second largest city. Through a careful interview with each of them, he asked about their living conditions, earnings and life satisfaction. Each were shown a card with a series of faces from sad to smiling, matched with seven descriptions from "very unhappy" to "very happy."

The results were sensational: 70% of the trash pickers reported feeling generally happy. Half scored themselves in the top two categories of "very happy" or "quite happy." Just 4% said they were "very unhappy" – far lower than the average American.[16] Even more astonishing was the revelation that there was no correlation between happiness and their incomes. The ones who earned more each month were no happier than those struggling below the poverty line. Don't forget, this was an independent researcher going into the slums to speak with some of the most stigmatized labourers in one of the poorest cities on earth. The trash pickers had no possible reason to lie. They appeared to fully understand the question – but no one had ever asked them before.

These results seem startling; they may make for uncomfortable reading. After all, there's a huge debate going on across the world about living wages and pay differentials. As we'll see later on, pay *does matter* for some living in extreme poverty, below the breadline, who cannot meet basic needs. But this research questions how *much* pay matters compared to other factors when it comes to wellbeing.

Why did the Nicaraguan trash pickers say they were so happy? Clearly, their lack of money was not preventing positive feelings about life. Over two-thirds were married or in a relationship; most had children. A clear majority said they were happy with their relationships with friends, families and co-workers in the skips. Interestingly, those who said they regularly took part in sports (slum games such as soccer and baseball) were significantly more likely to be content. Most described themselves as in a good state of health.

Above all, the trash pickers appeared to be optimists. When asked about their outlook for the future, 70% said they thought it would be "better than the present." Similar research in 11 African countries found that the poorest are often the most optimistic. It's when a country develops and the middle class swells that pessimism sets in. This may be because optimism is a survival mechanism on the poverty line, or perhaps because many reach the conclusion that life can only get better.[17]

These findings are profound and controversial. As the Spanish researcher who uncovered them concluded, they challenge the widespread assumption that well-paid, quality work is essential for wellbeing. Despite the unsavoury conditions in the garbage heaps of Nicaragua, good relationships make for a happy community. You might think that the findings are just an isolated example, a quirk amid vast swathes of poverty that causes misery. After all, don't we keep hearing that businesses are paying the rich bosses too much, and the poorest in their operations and supply chains too little?

As Richard Easterlin identified, there is no doubt that wealthier countries are, on average, happier than very poor ones. Wealthier people *within* countries are also happier. But the relationship is not linear, and the effects fade away as people move up the income ladder. Just because a country and its workers get wealthier, it doesn't mean the residents will get any happier.[18]

In Mexico, for example, rising incomes have been shown to have a limited impact on life satisfaction. Personal relationships, on the other hand, have a very powerful effect.[19] Another study of workers in clothing sweatshops in India found "no relationship between actual income and satisfaction with life."[20] So, the experience of the Nicaraguan trash pickers is not unique. Study after study has found that even among the very poorest, money accounts for a very small proportion of what statisticians call the variance in happiness.[21] Above about $5,000 GNP per capita, wellbeing shows no correlation with income levels around the world.[22]

In the next chapter, we'll examine some more examples from the supply chain industries of the developing world. We'll discover what business can really do to make a difference to life satisfaction. But the key point for now is that, in the words of one scholar who has studied this, "a person with very low income is not necessarily unhappy."[23]

There is one group for whom income really does matter: those who cannot afford the basic necessities in life.[24] No one can be happy without the essentials for survival, such as food, water and a place to sleep. This is why many advocate that the greatest gains in wellbeing can come from increasing the incomes of the very lowest paid.[25]

Although money matters in some situations, it is rarely the solution to raising wellbeing for those above the poverty line.[26] Above a certain pay level, rewarding farmers, truck drivers, factory workers or sales teams more and more financially won't *necessarily* make them feel any happier. Sure, for some individuals, it might. But for most people, over time, it won't. If we want to work out how business can raise wellbeing, a host of factors besides how much people are paid explain most of the opportunities. Money is only one part of the puzzle.

Money as part of life

What things in life really matter to you? In surveys asking this type of question, money *never* comes top. It doesn't even rank particularly highly. Good health, close family and friends, and dignity and respect crop up much more often.[27] When the UK Government asked this exact question in a public consultation, it received 34,000 responses. Health, getting along with friends and relatives, the environment, education and training, and cultural activities such as volunteering all ranked higher than income and wealth. Economic security and job satisfaction cropped up, but actual pay levels were surprisingly unimportant.[28]

In the workplace, how valued and respected we feel, as well as our type of work, relationships with colleagues and work–life balance, score higher than salary in most studies. Bonuses actually came bottom of the Mercer global engagement survey – based on the views of thousands of workers in the US, UK, China, Japan, India, Germany and France.[29]

The reason why money doesn't explain our happiness is that incomes are only one part of life. Salaries are only one part of the job. In the previous chapter, we looked at the different domains that influence how we answer those "satisfied with life" questions. The domains include satisfaction with our financial situation, occupation, health, relationships and so on.

Some fascinating research has explored how rising pay affects the different domains. Of all the areas where you'd expect money to help, you might reckon that higher incomes improve how people feel about their *financial* situation. But this simply isn't the case. The correlation between pay and economic satisfaction is remarkably low. Some people on high salaries feel they don't have enough while others on lower pay are quite content. There is no clear pattern.[30]

What about the other domains of life? Do those with higher wages have better job satisfaction, or health, or relationships with loved ones? In actual fact, more money often makes us feel *less* happy with these other aspects. Take the example of job satisfaction. Does pay increase happiness with work? It appears not. One review of 92 studies involving 15,000 individuals over 120 years found just a 2% overlap between pay and job satisfaction.[31] That's startlingly low. You are much more likely to value your job if you do it because you enjoy it, not because it pays well. Those in better-paid jobs often have more responsibility and pressure. This can raise anxiety, working hours and commute times.[32] Overall, higher-paid workers don't seem to have any higher occupational satisfaction than lower-paid ones.[33]

But it's life outside of the workplace that is affected the most by money.[34] Just think of the stressed executive with no time for family. Or the exhausted on-call doctor whose own health begins to suffer. Rising income has also been linked to higher divorce rates[35] and less enjoyment with the little things in life.[36]

The relationship between money and all the other things that make life worthwhile is astonishingly small. It's practically random in most studies, meaning money simply doesn't matter. If you stop to think about it, this makes perfect sense. Why should a bigger pay packet make our friendships any stronger?

For some, higher incomes might lead to better health if you can afford to live somewhere greener, or buy medicines or a personal trainer. For others, higher-paid work might mean more stress and long hours in a sedentary, isolated job fuelled by junk food. This will have the opposite effect. Someone else might be dissatisfied with their pay packet but enjoy fantastic health and brilliant relationships, and so feel very happy overall.[37]

The weak link between pay and happiness is also evident for the very poorest. Someone might be classified as living in income poverty but experience happiness in other domains of life. That's exactly what we found with the Nicaraguan trash pickers whose health, families and friendships were strong. It's not just that wealth is relative. It's not just that we adapt to income, or even that sometimes the poorest have lower expectations from life. It's rather that money is not the only thing that explains quality of life.[38] As Professor Mariano Rojas has concluded from studies in Mexico:

> People do not only consume, but they also have partners and children, enjoy or get bored with their use of free time, feel the distress of not having enough time to enjoy their hobbies and to pursue their interests, have friends and neighbors whom they share life with . . . occupy their days in many activities, and face health-related problems. Hence, the weak relationship between overall happiness and income should come as no surprise once it is realized that overall happiness measures refer to the well-being of persons, and not to the well-being of consumers.[39]

In recent years, the responsible business agenda has focused more on money. Issues such as living wages in supply chains, astronomical executive rewards and gender pay gaps have all risen up the agenda. But the point that's been missing is that it's not how much you pay, but how it affects life, that counts. Pay differentials matter because they perpetuate feelings of unfairness and dissatisfaction.

Money is never the whole story. Focusing on wages at the expense of all the other things that make life worth living is also a recipe for misery. In the grand scheme of life, salaries and bonuses appear to be one of the *least* important contributions that business makes to wellbeing. While wages are essential to the very poorest who cannot meet basic needs, they are a very small part of the wellbeing footprint. Income simply cannot explain large parts of the variations in life satisfaction felt by suppliers, employees and consumers. But if you think all this means that companies can't do anything about pay to improve life satisfaction, think again. There are clear steps that any business can take to ensure that salaries help, rather than hinder, happiness.

A fair play plan

Google encourages its staff to embrace radical innovation. But in July 2015, one employee went a bit too far. Erica Baker embarked on a dramatic experiment in transparency. She set up a spreadsheet and encouraged her colleagues to add some previously secret information: how much they were paid.

Her idea took off like wildfire, she later recalled. Using the Twitter pseudonym of @EricaJoy, she told the story of how colleagues started adding more details, such as what bonuses they'd got from Google's peer-review system. Managers had to approve these awards. Erica alleged that her bonuses had been blocked – something that as a black woman in a white, male-dominated industry provoked a massive online storm. It also caused a raucous inside the company. Erica's spreadsheet reportedly caused huge numbers of Google employees to challenge their pay and bonuses. By the time she left, it was estimated that 5% of the entire workforce had shared their salaries on her spreadsheet.[40]

Although employees have a legal right to share and discuss salary information under federal law in the US, this tale shows just how controversial wages can be. What Erica uncovered was a perceived lack of fairness. Whether or not we feel something is just matters enormously for wellbeing. One study following young Australians as they entered the workforce found that how satisfied they *felt* with their pay was much more important to happiness than their actual earnings.[41] Perceptions are critical.

A Wellthy Company approaches pay in a way that is perceived as balanced and fair by employees. Contracts of employment are particularly important, and need to be reasonable in the eyes of those signing them. When people feel that they are treated fairly, they have higher job satisfaction, better health, and are more committed to the company. They also perform better and are more likely to behave in an ethical manner.[42] Part of this is consistency. Take bonuses. Research shows that small bonuses, given erratically from one year to the next, can actually be worse for wellbeing than no bonuses at all.[43]

The second issue is inequality. Since the global financial crisis, astronomical executive bonuses for mediocre performance have been in the firing line. While some studies have found that greater income inequality decreases wellbeing, others have found no clear link.[44] As we'll see in Chapter 7, the important thing is for business to contribute to a culture of high trust and mutual cooperation. This requires keeping a watch on excessive pay gaps – a sense check on pay cheques. Salary ratios should be calculated, such as between the highest and lowest earners. Disclosing these data helps to ensure that senior management's remuneration is not vastly out of kilter with the rest of the business and society.

The real reason why pay matters is because it sends a signal. Salaries send a message about status. Our position in the pecking order matters inordinately for happiness. It's not our absolute or relative pay that really counts, but where we rank in the organizational hierarchy.[45] If we think we stack up well on the pay scale, we are much more likely to be satisfied with life.[46]

A Wellthy Company cannot make everyone top dog. Even the flattest organizational structures still require some hierarchy. But a business can create meaning and status for each member of staff, and show that they are valued and respected, by giving more than money.

The gift of anything but money

Posters appeared on the university campus advertising a menial task: library books had to be catalogued. But behind this innocuous call was a clever experiment. Would people work harder for more pay or a tacky gift? In this study from Germany, students who signed up were told that they would receive €12 per hour. Upon arrival, one group were told that they were getting a surprise 20% pay rise. Another group were shown a thermos flask (equivalent in value to a 20% rise) that was wrapped in transparent gift paper. They were told that this was to be their bonus. A third control group was given no extra pay and no gift. What impact would this have on how quickly they catalogued the books?

The unexpected cash had absolutely no effect on productivity. They worked just as hard (or slowly) as the students on €12 an hour. But the surprise gift caused a 25% increase in efficiency. They literally typed in a quarter as many books simply because they'd been promised a cheap plastic thermos.

Non-financial rewards such as tacky bottles, more holiday time, flexible working and recognition from colleagues have a much more substantial and lasting impact on how we feel than money. Professor Tim Kasser, an expert on psychology and wellbeing, has worked out that when offered a pay rise, most people should request more holiday instead.[47] Time off work is likely to boost happiness more than extra pay – something we'll return to later in the book.

Most people believe that more pay will make them happier. Asked to pick, the German students demanded more money, rather than the bottle. It's often the signal that's sent by an employer that matters the most. In studies looking into this, the more care and attention given to a benefit, the bigger an impact it has. Provided salaries are seen as fair, then carefully chosen, thoughtful and personalized rewards are a far better way to make staff happier than more money.

Finally, the worst thing that a business can do is to cut pay. Needless to say, reducing salaries is a rapid route to distress and unhappiness. The need for income to be secure is often more important than its amount. In one amazing study, income uncertainty was shown to reduce wellbeing more powerfully than very strong physical pain.[48] Another found that a fall in income hurts twice as much as an equal rise helps happiness.[49] So even though increasing pay doesn't lead to more happiness, it doesn't mean that reducing pay won't have the reverse affect.

What is money for?

The scant evidence of a link between higher pay and happiness shouldn't come as any great surprise. Our celebrity-obsessed culture paints a picture of money (and fame) as the pinnacles of life. But as psychologists, artists and religious leaders have preached for centuries, you simply can't buy happiness.

What purpose does money serve? Economists used to say that wealth was the means by which we revealed our preferences. The amount we are prepared to work for, and what we spend our cash on, explains how much the job or a product means to us. Adam Smith's hidden hand guides us in pure self-interest.

But is money the best insight into what we value in life? Does the amount for which we'll work really indicate what makes us happiest? As we've seen, there are plenty of super-wealthy individuals who are stressed and miserable, and there are stigmatized, poverty-stricken trash pickers who rate their life satisfaction remarkably highly.

Money matters because it is a means to something else – one lever that can help, or hinder, our search for a happy life. For most people, the actual job and what goes with it (status, fairness, respect and those non-financial rewards and recognition) are vastly more important for wellbeing than the salary level. The funny thing is that classical economists knew that wealth was not the goal, but merely a step on the way to wellbeing. As the noted Alfred Marshall wrote in 1890:

> Economics is a study of mankind in the ordinary business of life; it examines . . . the attainment and . . . use of the material requisites of wellbeing. Thus it is on the one side a study of wealth; and on the other, and more important side, a part of the study of man.[50]

In other words, economics is not about money. It's about people, and the choices we make for our wellbeing. Over 100 years later, perhaps we are just getting back to the roots of what prosperity is all about.

To summarize, then, if our starting point is: do the wages that companies pay matter? The answer is yes, partially – but not as much as you might think. They matter in terms of fairness, and in a relative sense. They matter if they are cut. They matter for the very poorest who cannot afford basic needs. But otherwise, health and relationships, flexibility and free time, dignity and recognition, and stimulation and challenge are much more critical. We'll delve into the secrets to boosting happiness at work in the following chapters.

If we flip the question around and ask: from all the ways that businesses make people feel better and worse about life, what's most important? If truth be told, it's rarely money. To uncover the factors that really better life, we must begin our journey higher up the supply chain with a visit to a gigantic factory in China.

Notes

1 Mill, J. S. (1907). Posthumous essay on social freedom, *Oxford and Cambridge Review*, June, cited in Pigou, A. C. (1920). *The Economics of Welfare*. London: Macmillan.
2 Brickman, P., Coates, D. & Janoff-Bulman, R. (1978). Lottery winners and accident victims: is happiness relative? *Journal of Personality and Social Psychology*, *36*(8), 917–927.
3 Easterlin, R. A. (2004). The economics of happiness. *Daedalus*, *133*(2), 26–33.
4 Easterlin, R. A. (1974). Does economic growth improve the human lot? In P. A. David and M. W. Reder (eds.), *Nations and Households in Economic Growth: Essays in Honour of Moses Abramovitz* (pp. 89–125). New York: Academic Press.
5 Veenhoven, R. (2004). *Sustainable Consumption and Happiness*. Rotterdam: Erasmus University.
6 Diener, E., Sandvik, E., Seidlitz, L. & Diener, M. (1993). The relationship between income and subjective well-being: relative or absolute? *Social Indicators Research*, *28*(3), 195–223.
7 Bentham, J. (1952). The philosophy of economic science. *Jeremy Bentham's Economic Writings*, *1*, 81–119.
8 Frey, B. S. & Stutzer, A. (2002). What can economists learn from happiness research? *Journal of Economic literature*, *40*(2), 402–435; Diener, E. & Biswas-Diener, R. (2011). *Happiness: Unlocking the Mysteries of Psychological Wealth*. New York: John Wiley & Sons.
9 Easterlin, R. A. (2004). The economics of happiness. *Daedalus*, *133*(2), 26–33.
10 Clark, A. E. & Oswald, A. J. (1996). Satisfaction and comparison income. *Journal of Public Economics*, *61*(3), 359–381.
11 Montero, R. & Vásquez, D. (2015). Job satisfaction and reference wages: evidence for a developing country. *Journal of Happiness Studies*, *16*(6), 1493–1507.
12 Clark, A. & Senik, C. (2010). Who compares to whom? The anatomy of income comparisons in Europe. *The Economic Journal*, *120*(544), 573–594.
13 On bonuses, see Pouliakas, K. (2010). Pay enough, don't pay too much or don't pay at all? The impact of bonus intensity on job satisfaction. *Kyklos*, *63*(4), 597–626.
14 Knight, J. & Gunatilaka, R. (2012). Aspirations, adaptation and subjective well-being of rural–urban migrants in China. In D. A. Clarke (ed.), *Adaptation, Poverty and Development* (pp. 91–110). London: Palgrave Macmillan.
15 Diener, E., Horwitz, J. & Emmons, R. A. (1985). Happiness of the very wealthy. *Social Indicators Research*, *16*(3), 263–274.
16 Smith, T. et al. (2015). *General Social Surveys, 1972–2012: Cumulative*. Chicago, IL: NORC at the University of Chicago.
17 Graham, C. (2012). *Happiness around the World: The Paradox of Happy Peasants and Miserable Millionaires*. Oxford: Oxford University Press.
18 Easterlin, R. (n.d.). *Easterlin: Why There Is Still a Paradox*. Retrieved 12 November 2016, from www.nationalaccountsofwellbeing.org/learn/need/easterlin-still-challenge.html.
19 Rojas, M. (2011). Happiness, income, and beyond. *Applied Research in Quality of Life*, *6*(3), 265–276.

20 Dickson, M. A. & Littrell, M. A. (2003). Measuring quality of life of apparel workers in Mumbai, India: integrating quantitative and qualitative data on basic minimum needs, living wages, and well-being. In M. J. Sirgy, D. Rahtz & A. C. Samli (eds.), *Advances in Quality-of-Life Theory and Research* (pp. 211–232). Dordrecht: Springer.

21 Diener, E., Sandvik, E., Seidlitz, L. & Diener, M. (1993). The relationship between income and subjective well-being: relative or absolute? *Social Indicators Research, 28*(3), 195–223; Rojas, M. (2011). Happiness, income, and beyond. *Applied Research in Quality of Life, 6*(3), 265–276.

22 Frey, B. S. & Stutzer, A. (2002). What can economists learn from happiness research? *Journal of Economic literature, 40*(2), 402–435.

23 Rojas, M. (2011). Happiness, income, and beyond. *Applied Research in Quality of Life, 6*(3), 265–276.

24 This is supported by the UK Government's national wellbeing studies, as well as, for example, Graham, C. (2012). *Happiness around the World: The Paradox of Happy Peasants and Miserable Millionaires.* Oxford: Oxford University Press.

25 New Economics Foundation (2014). *Wellbeing at Work: A Review of the Literature.* London: New Economics Foundation.

26 Some scholars have contested the findings – arguing that increased income does indeed raise life satisfaction, but not emotional happiness day-to-day. See Kahneman, D. & Deaton, A. (2010). High income improves evaluation of life but not emotional well-being. *Proceedings of the National Academy of Sciences, 107*(38), 16489–16493.

27 Chambers, R. (1997). *Whose Reality Counts? Putting the First Last.* London: Intermediate Technology Publications (ITP).

28 Evans, J. (2011). *Findings from the National Well-Being Debate.* London: Office for National Statistics.

29 Cited in Cooper, C. L. & Wood, S. (2011). Happiness at work: why it counts. *The Guardian*, 15 July. Retrieved 22 December 2016, from www.theguardian.com/money/2011/jul/15/happiness-work-why-counts.

30 Easterlin, R. A. & Sawangfa, O. (2010). Happiness and economic growth: does the cross section predict time trends? Evidence from developing countries. In E. Diener, J. F. Helliwell & D. Kahneman (eds.), *International Differences in Well-Being* (pp. 166–216). New York: Oxford University Press; Rojas, M. (2011). Happiness, income, and beyond. *Applied Research in Quality of Life, 6*(3), 265–276.

31 Judge, T. A., Piccolo, R. F., Podsakoff, N. P., Shaw, J. C. & Rich, B. L. (2010). The relationship between pay and job satisfaction: a meta-analysis of the literature. *Journal of Vocational Behavior, 77*(2), 157–167.

32 Bryson, A., Barth, E. & Dale-Olsen, H. (2012). Do higher wages come at a price? *Journal of Economic Psychology, 33*(1), 251–263; Kahneman, D., Krueger, A. B., Schkade, D., Schwarz, N. & Stone, A. A. (2006). Would you be happier if you were richer? A focusing illusion. *Science, 312*(5782), 1908–1910.

33 Leontaridi, R. M. & Sloane, P. J. (2004). Low pay, higher pay, earnings mobility and job satisfaction in Britain. In D. Meulders, R. Plasman & F. Rycx (eds.), *Minimum Wages, Low Pay and Unemployment* (pp. 87–140). London: Palgrave Macmillan.

34 Caza, B. & Wrzesniewski, A. (2013). How work shapes well-being. In S. A. David, I. Boniwell & A. C. Ayers (eds.), *The Oxford Handbook of Happiness* (pp. 693–710). Oxford: Oxford University Press.

35 Clydesdale, T. T. (1997). Family behaviors among early US baby boomers: exploring the effects of religion and income change, 1965–1982. *Social Forces, 76*(2), 605–635.

36 Brickman, P., Coates, D. & Janoff-Bulman, R. (1978). Lottery winners and accident victims: is happiness relative? *Journal of Personality and Social Psychology*, *36*(8), 917–927.

37 Rojas, M. (2011). Happiness, income, and beyond. *Applied Research in Quality of Life*, *6*(3), 265–276.

38 Rojas, M. (2007). A subjective well-being equivalence scale for Mexico: estimation and poverty and income-distribution implications. *Oxford Development Studies*, *35*(3), 273–293.

39 Rojas, M. (2011). Happiness, income, and beyond. *Applied Research in Quality of Life*, *6*(3), 265–276.

40 Weinberger, M. (2015). Engineer says Google managers denied her bonuses when she tried to expose salary inequality. *Business Insider*, 18 July. Retrieved 1 February 2017, from http://uk.businessinsider.com/erica-baker-pay-inequality-at-google-2015-7?r=US&IR=T; Guynn, J. (2015). Ex-Google employee alleges unequal pay. *USA Today*, 21 July. Retrieved 1 February 2017, from www.usatoday.com/story/tech/2015/07/21/former-google-employee-alleges-unequal-pay/30481175/.

41 Dockery, A. M. (2005). The happiness of young Australians: empirical evidence on the role of labour market experience. *Economic Record*, *81*(255), 322–335.

42 Caza, B. & Wrzesniewski, A. How work shapes well-being. In S. A. David, I. Boniwell & A. C. Ayers (eds.), *The Oxford Handbook of Happiness* (pp. 693–710). Oxford: Oxford University Press.

43 Pouliakas, K. (2010). Pay enough, don't pay too much or don't pay at all? The impact of bonus intensity on job satisfaction. *Kyklos*, *63*(4), 597–626.

44 For a discussion on income inequality and happiness, see Pinker, S. (2018). *Enlightenment Now*. New York: Random House.

45 Brown, G. D., Gardner, J., Oswald, A. J. & Qian, J. (2008). Does wage rank affect employees' well-being? *Industrial Relations: A Journal of Economy and Society*, *47*(3), 355–389.

46 Boyce, C. J., Brown, G. D. & Moore, S. C. (2010). Money and happiness: rank of income, not income, affects life satisfaction. *Psychological Science*, *21*(4), 471–475.

47 Kasser, T. (2003). *The High Price of Materialism*. Cambridge, MA: MIT Press.

48 Cummins, R., Woerner, J., Tomyn, A., Gibson, A. & Knapp, T. M. (2006). *Wellbeing of Australians: Income Security*. Victoria: Australian Centre on Quality of Life.

49 Data from Annex 4.1 that accompanies Layard, R. (2011). *Happiness: Lessons from a New Science*. London: Penguin.

50 Marshall, A. (1890). *Principles of Economics: An Introductory Volume* (8th edition). London: Macmillan, p. 871.

Chapter 4

Source

Supply chain satisfaction

> No society can surely be flourishing and happy, of which the far greater part of the members are poor and miserable.
>
> Adam Smith (1723–1790)[1]

It was around 8 a.m. on 17 March 2010 when a young girl threw herself from her bedroom window. Tian Yu fell four storeys to the ground outside the factory where she worked and slept. After a 14-day coma, she emerged with a fractured spine and hips. The 17-year-old was left paralysed from the waist down. She survived to tell a heart-rending story of the human cost of brutal toil in multinational supply chains.[2]

The teenager was an employee at Foxconn's Longhua plant in Shenzhen, China. She had been employed for just 37 days making Apple iPhones and iPads. She is typical of a generation of young women and men who have left their families and rural life to gamble on a hope.

"Hurry towards your finest dreams, pursue a magnificent life," urged the employee handbook that she was given on arrival. But Tian Yu was not able to pursue her magnificent dream of a happier life. Instead, she experienced a system of inhumane efficiency. A typical day was 12 hours long with apparently mandatory overtime. The working week was six days. Toilet breaks and chatting on the production line were strictly controlled. After all, she had a quota to meet, checking iPhone screens for cracks. Even the way in which she had to sit was obsessively standardized.

Posters on the workshop walls ranged from the bizarre ("Growth, thy name is suffering; a harsh environment is a good thing") to the ominous ("Achieve goals or the sun will no longer rise"). Each morning, managers would start the day with a ritual of shouting at employees, "How are you?". The workers would chant in unison, "Good! Very good! Very, very good!"

But life was not good for Tian Yu. With little training and no emotional support, the final straw came when the Longhua system failed to produce her first pay packet. Distraught, exhausted and highly stressed, the teenager decided to take her own life. Despite the relentless automation of humans at Longhua, the tragic irony is that the system couldn't even pay this teenager what she was owed.

But what makes this story so devastating is that Tian Yu is by no means unique. Eighteen other workers at the same factory attempted suicide that year. Fourteen of them were successful. Foxconn, the factory owner, faced public outrage across the world. They scrambled to minimize the damage to their reputation – and that of their major customer, Apple. Foxconn made the extraordinary claim that the suicide rate at their factories was below the average in China of 23 deaths for every 100,000 people.[3] Suicide nets now drape beneath the windows to prevent Tian Yu's colleagues from following her and turning their backs on the Foxconn dream.

The globalization of supply chains has spawned hundreds of millions of new jobs like Tian Yu's. The Longhua factory employs an astonishing 400,000 workers. That's more than the entire population of a city such as New Orleans or Florence. Imagine the bustle and excitement of the new arrivals, most just 20 years of age, who have left their families to seek their fortune in this giant factory-cum-city.

Every day, young migrants across the developing world arrive by their thousands at city-factories such as Longhua. They assemble our gadgets, package our foods and stitch our clothes. Further up the supply chain, they mine minerals, chop forests and tend crops. Can they all be as unhappy as Tian Yu? If you read the stories in the media and follow the campaigns by non-governmental organizations (NGOs), you'll have seen tales of degrading conditions, unsafe practices and human rights abuses. But workers keep migrating to mining towns, plodding through plantations and sweating in sweatshops. Why do so few turn their back on the dream?

The human side of supply networks

The supply and distribution networks of multinationals criss-cross the world in an elaborate web of lives. When a company sources its palm oil, potatoes or packaging from the developing world, the potential to improve lives and grow wellbeing is immense.

It's been estimated that half a billion people work in such industries: digging up and chopping down raw materials from the earth, planting and harvesting, fishing, and sewing, stitching, moulding, soldering, assembling, painting and packaging goods for export.

Here's a little exercise that brings the human side of this to life. Try to picture the people involved in creating this book for a moment. If you're holding a paper copy, imagine where the pulp might have originated. What do the people look like who might have felled the tree, processed, inked, boxed and transported it to you? Are they happy?

The answer is probably not. Gallup, the polling company, asks people whether they do something interesting and like what they do at work each day. Those working in agriculture, fishing and forestry score the very lowest; just 11% are thriving, globally, according to this measure.[4] This is a massive tragedy for all companies that buy these commodities – and a major opportunity for pioneering businesses to make a difference.

If you are holding an e-reader or tablet, the story is even more interesting. The circuitry, plastic, microchips and battery each have an extraordinary tale of their own. It starts down a mine, with someone digging up a rare component such as tantalum, perhaps from the war-torn Democratic Republic of Congo. This super-resistant metal is used in computers, phones, medical devices and DVD players. But it's a conflict mineral that's been linked to wars and serious human rights abuses. People such as Tian Yu then helped to mould, shape, solder, assemble, check and package your electrophoretic display.

A human web of workshops, factories, warehouses and packaging centres make up the vital organs of the supply network. Those working in transport are the life-blood that connects the organs, pumping parts and products through the system by bike and car, truck and boat, train and cargo plane.

Our whistle-stop tour of logistics ends with retail. After the product has been manufactured, it's normally sold to you and me through a shop or website. We've all heard of Walmart and Amazon. But for everyday purchases, it might be your local store. In the developing world, many snacks, drinks and small household products are sold by entrepreneurial men and women from carts and makeshift huts beside roads, tracks and beaches. Even in the deepest forests of our planet, you can still buy a Coca-Cola or Colgate toothpaste. There is a particularly exciting opportunity for businesses to create worthwhile jobs in these informal distribution networks.

What's a job worth?

Economists used to say that the measure of whether someone liked their job was whether they stuck at it. The free market of labour dictates that supply matches demand. People move in response to what they are prepared to put up with. If the jobs at Longhua weren't better than life on the family farmstead, people would simply leave the horrors of the factory and return to the countryside.

The reality is not so simple. There are all sorts of reasons why migrants don't turn their back on export production and city life – even if the conditions turn out to be appalling. The massive distances that many migrate within and between countries is one barrier. Bonded contacts – forms of modern slavery in some cases – mean workers are in punitive levels of debt to their new masters and people traffickers. The fear of shaming a family back home also leads many to stay, no matter how tough, and fight for the dream of a better life.

To understand what a job is really worth to anyone, we need to unpick which aspects elevate and erode their happiness. For companies sourcing materials from the developing world, the challenges and opportunities are immense. We need to examine the real evidence on what does and does not affect life satisfaction. But the conventional criteria used to judge success in supply chains seem to obscure wellbeing.

New metrics for procurement

The relationship between a business and its suppliers used to come down to cost, time and quality. Can the procurement team get the parts needed, as quickly as possible, to the required standard at the lowest cost? Nowadays, most multinationals weigh up a more complex set of criteria, including the reliability and resilience of logistics, as well as traceability, which basically means whether you work out where each part has come from.

The rise of corporate responsibility has created a phenomenal industry of supplier standard setters and checkers. Inspections assess whether working conditions are safe, human rights are respected and environmentally sensitive processes are used. Every year, many thousands of audits are undertaken to try to ensure that promises are being kept.[5]

Cost, time and quality are no longer the only things that matter in logistics. But all the codes, checks and audits are no good unless we are clear about what we are trying to achieve. What we surely desire is for those working in supply chains to have basic rights, safe conditions and environmentally responsible practices because these things *make life better today* and for future generations. An ethical supply chain should be about boosting of life satisfaction. But how many auditors ask about happiness?

Poverty is not just about money

On a warm summer's day in 2010, shoppers on London's Old Kent Road were handed two 1 pence coins (about 3 US cents). They were told to go into Asda, the supermarket owned by Walmart, and give the money to the cashier. A coordinated campaign by ActionAid, an NGO, was seeking to highlight what they called "poverty wages" in Asda's garment sourcing. The two pennies were symbolic: it was the activists' best estimate of what would need to be added to a £4 ($5.60) T-shirt to double the wages of the garment worker that made them in Asia.[6]

But the campaigners also did something even sneakier. They went into Asda stores and slipped little notes about wages into the pockets of the clothes. Any shopper who found a leaflet was offered a free T-shirt as a prize – an elaborate treasure hunt to raise awareness of pay packets in far-flung factories.

This campaign was highly innovative and media-friendly. It's just one example of countless initiatives from increasingly savvy non-profits that target the big brands. It also highlights how many campaigns are increasingly homing in on just one issue: wages.

The global financial crisis of 2008 made the topic of pay all the more salient. Campaigners contrast massive pay packets awarded to executives with the "poverty wages" given to workers who made the products. The idea of a living wage has been rapidly gaining traction. This is pay that's above legal minimums and enough to cover the costs of housing, food and other bills in a local country or city.

Asda responded to the ActionAid campaign by decrying the research as "flawed." The supermarket pointed out that there was an incredibly complex set of issues involved in sourcing clothes from Asia, especially given the low prices needed to clothe poorer families in the West. The issues Asda listed included factory conditions, working hours and training.[7] Reading their response to the campaign, you can sense their frustration that their critics had simplified all the nuances of the supply chain down to the singular topic of salaries.

Poverty used to mean a lack of income. But since the early 1990s, the development field has undergone something of a slow revolution. There is an increasing recognition in academic circles that quality of life depends on so much more than money alone. Just as we saw with the trash pickers of Nicaragua in the previous chapter, unhappiness and deprivation are not the same things as income poverty. As the development expert Robert Chambers pointed out over 20 years ago, it's perfectly possible to have the highest income in your village but still lack adequate resources. You can also have very little money but a decent quality of life.[8]

The fruit farmers of Senegal

The fruit farmers of Senegal illustrate the point. In 2007, a team of researchers trudged along a slice of windswept coast known as Les Niayes. They knocked on the doors of the huts and shacks of nearly 500 farming households. Their mission: to find out how farming green beans and mangos for export affected quality of life.

The farmers were asked a series of questions about their household income, and whether they worked on commercial farms or small-scale family ones. But they were also asked a more profound query: "In general, are you happy?" The answers were scored on a five-point scale from "very unhappy" to "very happy." Once the data were crunched, the findings were consistent with others we have seen: household income bore no relation to how happy the farmers were.[9]

Further studies in supply chain industries have backed up these results. For example, among paddy farmers in Malaysia, government support, cooperation among peers and satisfaction with the work are stronger determinants of quality of life than income.[10] For a cross section of agricultural, mining, manufacturing and construction workers in rural Vietnam, only relative, not absolute, income matters.[11] In the developed world, a study of farmers in Northern Ireland found no clear relationship between household income and life satisfaction; again, other factors such as levels of education were more significant.[12]

We need to reiterate a note of caution here. There is no doubt that a lack of money is the primary cause of misery in many lives. Paying wages that are inadequate for even the basic necessities of life is a recipe not just for unhappiness, but quite possibly death. Hence, the toxic term that has been levelled by American politicians against some brands: "starvation wages."[13]

Back in the 1940s, the American psychologist Abraham Maslow proposed that we seek to satisfy physical needs (such as for food and safety) before personal and emotional ones.[14] Without a basic level of income, the lowest earners cannot feed their children, put a roof over their heads or access basic resources such as nutritious foods, safe drinking water, clean sanitation and life-saving medicines. All the other things that make for a happy life are irrelevant unless those on the breadline receive an adequate wage.

Among the very poorest households in Bangladesh, for example, significantly fewer people say they are happy with their lives. Farmers and transport workers are among the most miserable.[15] Studies of artisans enrolled in a fair trade scheme in Peru show that for those on the lowest incomes, pay is a key variable to raising happiness.[16]

For the very poorest, wages are vital for wellbeing. But the debate comes down to what constitutes a breadline level.[17] Some pioneers such as Unilever and H&M are already working this out and enforcing minimum levels among their suppliers.[18] Yet when it comes to life satisfaction, it's far too simplistic to conclude that just raising wages will make life better for those working in supply chains.

Amartya Sen, the Nobel Prize-winning economist, has championed the idea that quality of life for the poor is not adequately explained by income. Economic prosperity is just one pathway to improving life.[19] Sen's solution – a focus on what he terms "capabilities" – requires a more rounded approach to meeting their needs.[20] Some of his solutions are for governments, such as political freedoms. But many of them are issues that businesses can tackle, such as increasing access to finance, food, education and healthcare. The latest research on wellbeing shows that one particular capability does more to increase happiness than anything else: increasing access to worthwhile jobs.

Creating jobs in supply chains

Creating employment is the single most powerful means to raise life satisfaction in supply chains. As we saw in Chapter 2, jobs enhance self-esteem, strengthen personal networks and promote a feeling of control over life. This is particularly true of the world's poorest countries. In most cases, having any job – no matter what job – boosts wellbeing. As long as it pays a basic minimum wage, a job is better than unemployment.[21]

Of course, not all jobs are the same. The better the quality and more reliable a job, the better for wellbeing it will be. Those most satisfied with their experiences at work are typically more satisfied with life overall. But the key point is that it's the existence of the job itself that matters most.

A job can mean very different things to different people. In order to optimize the impact on life satisfaction, there is a twist to all this. A Wellthy Company creates jobs for *those who value them the most*. The business creates opportunities for the very poorest, women and minority groups to have a disproportionate impact on quality of life.

Imagine that getting a new job takes the average out-of-work city male from a 5 to a 7 (out of 10) on the life ladder that we looked at in Chapter 2. Now imagine that the starting point is not 5, but 3, for a mother who desperately needs work, but faces racial discrimination, perhaps in an isolated rural community. Now that very same opportunity, for a person with the same skills, might take the woman from a 3 to an 8. That's a transformational change to someone's life.

This jump from a job matters for two reasons. First, the starting score is lower. Within many developing countries, minorities are often the least happy groups.[22] Second, the boost is bigger. For those that face hurdles to employment, the benefit from getting the job – the value it creates for that individual – is greater.

The gender divide illustrates this perfectly. Women face widespread disadvantage and discrimination across the world, particularly in poorer countries and especially in industries such as agriculture. Studies have shown that a woman getting a job typically results in significantly higher jumps in wellbeing than a man would experience. This is perhaps because women's expectations from work are lower than men's.[23] Men have been running organizations and employing other men for 10,000 years, and seem subconsciously to have high expectations for patriarchy to continue.

Conversely, women appear, on average, to value the opportunity more. Some businesses have cottoned on to this opportunity, recognizing the benefits from investing in women as employees and suppliers. It's been estimated, for example, that women in developing countries reinvest about 90% of their income in their families. The equivalent for men is about 30–40%.[24]

Global food business Mars has established agricultural programmes that specifically source commodities from female smallholder farmers. Walmart, the world's largest retailer, has introduced a pioneering "women-owned" label for products bought from female-run suppliers.[25] Lots of companies talk about their social impact, but few think through how to really maximize it. The Wellbeing Purpose is about creating jobs across the supply network that are targeted at those who will benefit the most from them.

The same thinking applies not just to groups such as women or the rural poor, but whole countries. How about prioritizing buying from regions where wellbeing is lowest? Some of the poorest countries in the world, such as Burundi, Burkina Faso and Benin, consistently come bottom of the league tables of happiness. Cotton is grown in all three of these nations. For a Wellthy Company in the textiles business, procurement from these countries would be a top priority. Remember, the benefits are greatest where the starting point is most desperate.

There is a moral case for job creation in countries and communities where unhappiness is most endemic. But there is also a business one. Those given work who might otherwise lack it don't just get happier. They are also most likely to work hard to keep their opportunities. A study from Russia in the late 1990s found that happier people tend to earn more money and perform better in the labour market in future years – an effect felt most strongly for those on the lowest incomes.[26] In the next chapter, we'll look at the evidence showing that happier people perform better at work. Take just one example from a Chinese factory. Higher levels of hope, optimism and resilience among workers has been shown to be strongly correlated with higher productivity as rated by supervisors.[27] Happier workers are almost always more productive than unhappy ones.

For a Wellthy Company thinking about procurement policies, there is a strong alignment here. Wealth creation for shareholders and wellbeing creation for communities can go hand in hand. Suppliers who are happier are more reliable and more productive, and this can help to lower risks and increase margins. Improving productivity benefits the business while also improving life for many who would otherwise be very unhappy.

Although there are great challenges in sourcing from countries without the infrastructure and quality checks that established players have, the benefits of a long-term investment can pay off. Making procurement decisions to create the "greatest happiness of the greatest number," as Jeremy Bentham put it, could make great business sense. Yet we know that not all jobs are equal. As well as sheer numbers, there is another crucial component to ensure happiness in supply chains. To find out the answer, we must continue our journey across Africa and visit the oil palm farmers of Ghana.

The key to happiness for Ghanaian oil palm farmers

Around half the goods we use every day contain palm oil.[28] The oils are used to make foods such as margarine and chocolate, as well as cosmetics, candles and even laundry detergents. This phenomenal commodity is mired in huge controversies because of its impact on deforestation. But the story of its impact on happiness is less well known.

Ghana has been exporting palm oil for nearly 200 years. Around 80% of the crop comes from small-scale farmers.[29] Just as we've seen in other countries, studies of rural Ghanaians have found that strong community ties, access to water and the act of working – rather than wealth itself – affect wellbeing the most. While money can create "momentary happiness" for Ghanaians, income levels show a weak relationship with wellbeing.[30]

But amid these palm oil communities, one research project has discovered a fascinating factor with a striking correlation with happiness: formal contracts. Oil palm farmers with written deals to supply their crop turn out to be much happier with life than those in more precarious self-employment.[31]

It shouldn't come as a great surprise that job security is vital to feeling good about life. After all, how can anyone lead a happy existence if they don't know when the next pay cheque will come? Establishing formal contracts, particularly long-term ones, takes the pressure off suppliers. Reliability is the crucial complement to providing a job that's needed to grow wellbeing in supply chains.

In manufacturing "sweatshops," unstable employment is endemic. In Bangladesh, for example, some 75% of waged workers in the garment industry lack a formal contract.[32] Encouraged by NGOs and organizations such as the Ethical Trade Initiative, some companies have taken steps to reduce this type of precarious employment. For example, Adidas has a programme to increase the ratio of permanent to temporary workers among its suppliers.[33] Reliable jobs with formal contracts are the first steps. But there are other sources of pressure that need to be addressed too – some of which can have deadly consequences.

Lethal lead times

On 23 April 2013, workers at one factory making clothes for many high-street brands noticed large cracks in the walls. The shops and a bank on the ground floor were immediately evacuated as a precaution. Locals believed that the eight-storey building looked structurally unsafe. But the garment makers on the upper floors were in a different position. They were told to go back to work. After all, the factories had big contracts to supply brands such as Benetton in Italy, Cato Fashions and The Children's Place in the US and Matalan and Primark in the UK. Despite the apparent risk, management decreed that the day's orders had to be completed. Fast fashion couldn't wait.

The next day, the entire building crumbled in a lethal collapse. Bangladesh's Rana Plaza disaster was a devastation, taking 1,138 lives. Nearly 2,600 more people were injured, many of them maimed for the rest of their lives.[34]

It was the pressure to meet the day's orders that prompted managers to send workers back into the Rana Plaza factory. In the dizzy world of fast fashion, deadlines drive the decisions. Speed strains the system. Companies serious about wellbeing need to design and plan for stable lead times. In competitive clothing manufacture, this is a big challenge. Businesses must encourage safety and contentment in their supply networks by banning crazy lead times.

As well as reasonable deadlines, payments to suppliers must be prompt. If you are a small-scale farmer or artisan, a contract to supply a big company is only a legal promise to be paid in the future. It's cash that counts. Paying suppliers within a decent time period complements the stability and reliability of formal contracts. A relationship founded upon mutual respect can ensure a decent quality of life for suppliers.

Long-term relationships in the logistics network can make for more profitable business. By reducing the number of times that contracts are reviewed, and the paperwork of switching suppliers, set-up costs can be cut, price volatility minimized, and stronger relationships built.

By committing to a partnership over many years, not months, you can build mutual trust. That means both parties are more likely to invest in improvements such as training, safe in the knowledge that everyone's in it for the long haul. Making a commitment to suppliers can make great business sense and create more stability, and less risk, for the purchasing company. It also goes a long way towards helping those working in the developing world to plan for their future.

To summarize, then, wellbeing can be elevated in supply chains through creating worthwhile jobs where they matter the most, reliable contracts wherever possible, reasonable lead times, and prompt payments. It's not rocket science, but once we shift the focus away from simplistic slogans about pay and measure what improves people's life satisfaction, the answers are revealing, realistic and potentially life-changing.

Is small always best?

Both the Senegalese fruit and vegetable farmers and the Ghanaian oil palm farmers reveal something fascinating about size. Alongside being told to pay better wages, another big issue that campaigners lobby companies about is doing more to support small-scale enterprises.

Oxfam, for example, urges companies to "Think Big, Go Small." The romantic image of the self-sufficient farmer is contrasted with the big bad world of land-grabbing agri-firms, smiling cottage crafters are set against industrial sweatshops, and plucky street sellers battle with the retail giants. Is small best for happiness?

Some evidence suggests big is bad for wellbeing. For example, waged workers in Vietnam are much less happy than self-employed farmers.[35] Small can be more personal. Having a direct relationship with independent entrepreneurs can create more authentic and unique brands. It can result in better wellbeing if the relationships are managed judiciously. Fair trade cooperatives illustrate this perfectly, where wellbeing is typically much higher.[36]

Yet in the case of the Senegalese farmers, small is unhappy. The researchers found that while income didn't matter for happiness, self-employment did. Independent farmers were significantly *less* happy than those employed in the larger, agro-industrial farms.[37] In Ghana, the independent farmers were also less content than those on the formal outgrower scheme with a proper contract. This is because small often equates to unreliable and risky trade for suppliers. This means more stress, less ability to forward-plan, and so less happiness.

The truth is that the evidence is mixed in terms of whether small and independent is better for wellbeing. One small pilot study in Ethiopia found strong benefits to wellbeing from being given a job in a "sweatshop" compared to a cash grant for self-employment.[38] Yet a larger study by the same authors found no clear relationship, possibly because exposure to chemicals and fumes made the factory job less healthy.[39]

A review of multiple studies has found that the self-employed are happier, on average, in the US and Russia, but less happy in Latin America.[40] In the developing world, self-employment is often a necessity. If stable work isn't available, it can literally be for survival. In richer countries, working for yourself used to be considered a lifestyle choice. In the new gig economy of on-demand, often part-time workers, this is not always true. Happiness among freelance workers seems to depend on whether it's a career choice for more flexibility or a forced necessity for the money.[41]

This illustrates why sweeping generalizations such as "independent self-employment is best" or "formal employment is better" are misguided. If independent means a fear of being out of work, it's definitely not best for wellbeing. It's not the structure of the jobs that affect people's satisfaction with life. It's the reliability of their income and their experiences of the daily tasks involved.

Human rights and wellbeing wrongs

Over 20 years ago, a journalist by the name of Sydney Schanberg paid a visit to some workshops in a remote corner of Pakistan. What he found shocked the world: 12-year-old children squatting in shacks, stitching together footballs. The toys were being shipped to America for kids to do what kids should be doing: kicking the ball around outside, after a day at school.

"Do you want to go to school?" Sydney asked the children in one workshop. "Yes," came the quiet reply. But these children couldn't go to school. They had been bought for a few dollars from their parents, sold and resold, destined to years of enforced slavery. While Sydney's article in *Life* in 1996 mentioned Adidas and FIFA, the football governing body, one brand was struck so hard that it echoed through the ages: Nike.[42]

The public and political reaction was dramatic, bringing worldwide attention to the real-life stories behind Nike's supply chain. Within two years, Philip Knight, Nike's chairman and chief executive, admitted that "the Nike product has become synonymous with slave wages, forced overtime and arbitrary abuse . . . I truly believe that the American consumer does not want to buy products made in abusive conditions."[43]

This was without doubt one of the greatest corporate exposés in history. It shone a light on the shady corners of a multinational's supply network, illuminating misery and oppression that had been hidden from view. But it was the public's reaction that forced Nike to rethink human and labour rights. The firm began working with international bodies to create regulations banning child labour in Pakistan and supporting kids who had worked for their suppliers.[44]

It might sound obvious to state that fundamental freedoms and an absence of forced labour, violence and discrimination are essential for wellbeing to flourish. Oppression – whether caused by governments or supported by businesses – is one of the most potent causes of misery.[45] Industries at the top of the supply chain often face the most acute safety and human rights risks. According to one study of miners in Australia, improving working hours, accommodation standards, personal conflict and mental health does most to improve wellbeing.[46]

In any workplace, practices that promote safety and dignity create happier employees and a stronger work environment. The idea of decency at work should make sense for all companies in an age where transparency in the supply chain is changing so rapidly.

Edward Fisher, a professor of anthropology, has described how dignity and fairness are just as important to the wellbeing of the Guatemalan coffee farmer as to the German coffee drinker who frets over ethical sourcing.[47] Businesses need to put in place processes to identify and mitigate human rights issues in the supply chain, following a framework such as the United Nations Ruggie Principles.[48]

Mondelez International, a global foods company that makes Kenco coffee, has embraced a particularly innovative sourcing programme. *Coffee Made Happy* aims to do exactly that: source coffee beans from farmers in a way that makes everyone happier. It may sound twee, but there are rigorous targets behind the promise, including to help 1 million coffee farmers become successful entrepreneurs by 2020. The company makes the same link between the consumers' happiness and the suppliers' wellbeing. Mondelez says that "our coffee makes people happy" when they drink it, and they've extended that mission to the farmers who make the beans as well.

Coffee Made Happy is more than just a contract to supply beans to the business. It's an intensive programme of investment in skills such as bookkeeping and accounting, growing the self-confidence and respectability of farmers and securing a more reliable supply for the brands. Mondelez has set key performance indicators covering issues such as whether a career as a coffee farmer is respected in the communities that they source from.[49]

This example shows how multinationals can take a more rounded view of wellbeing in the supply chain. By investing in training, education and healthcare in local communities, brands can build strong social capital that is essential to well-functioning supply chains. Happier suppliers make for a more reliable network, and stronger ethics in sourcing can help sell brands too.

Environmental contentment

Alongside improving social standards, Mondelez's *Coffee Made Happy* also has a strand on environmental sustainability. Can greener practices really make farmers happier? The standard line with eco-initiatives is that it's all about the future. Managing resources such as water, minimizing greenhouse gas emissions and preserving vibrant habitats are all actions intended to grow the wellbeing of future generations. That's what environmental sustainability is all about – sustaining life's critical resources for the generations that follow.

But some studies suggest that there might be a more immediate link between greener behaviours and our happiness today. Researchers working with dairy farmers in New Zealand have discovered that organic farming is a strong contributor to feelings of personal wellbeing. Being in tune with the environment, and feeling part of something bigger, creates more positive emotions for farmers in their daily work.[50]

At an intuitive level, this seems logical: looking after the land might make our job seem more wholesome and worthwhile. It could even cause people to look after themselves more carefully too – and we know that good health, in turn, improves wellbeing. Air quality and pollution have been shown to have a marked effect on happiness.[51] Studies have also shown that exposure to parks with more butterflies – and even aquariums with more fish – can have a very immediate effect on our mood and health.[52]

The implications of this are quite profound. Rather than just talking about the future benefits of greener supply chains, a Wellthy Company can capitalize on more immediate ones. By looking at supplier practices with a wellbeing lens, it opens up opportunities to innovate radical new approaches to environmental responsibility. It's still early days, and there is more research to be done in this area. But a case could be made for joining the dots. Care for the environment might not be just for the happiness of our descendants. It could also raise the satisfaction of those working in agriculture, forestry, fishing and mining today.

These conclusions might seem unsurprising. It may sound obvious that secure employment that respects people and nature will increase wellbeing, whereas an unreliable income from unsafe, undignified and polluting work sows misery. But very few companies set out to measure and improve wellbeing in the supply chain. For all the audits and standards, only a tiny number of initiatives have attempted to measure how people feel about life and explore the difference that business can make.

The debates over pay and small-scale employment illustrate how wild generalizations can cause us to focus on the wrong issues. Companies wanting to take ethical sourcing seriously need to have a laser-like focus on enhancing life satisfaction. That should be the real objective of ethical supply chain management.

The lesson from Senegal's fruit and vegetable farmers, just like Ghana's oil palm farmers, is that providing a reliable income is one of the most influential interventions that corporate procurement can make. Pay levels matter to the very poorest, but any job with a reliable wage is the essential ingredient for most people's happiness. It's all too easy to be seduced by the romantic ideal that self-employment is always best. But a decent and steady income may trump an independent lifestyle if it results in wages that can be counted on and a more stable and safe working environment.

We can begin to see how the decisions made in sourcing – in what are often very long and complex networks – can grow wellbeing significantly. Across the world, in all workplaces, perceptions and experiences matter just as much as material living standards. Meaningful and healthy employment, strong social networks and personal autonomy matter the most wherever we work. What matters to the Senegalese farmer is not that different from the San Francisco shopper. It is a useful reminder to think of those whose lives are touched by any part of the business as humans – not workers or consumers, but people who are motivated and made happier by more than just money.[53]

Most CSR supply chain initiatives are all about the negatives: minimising risks, stopping abuses and tackling injustices. But employment should be about enjoyment. There has not been enough focus on the joys of work.[54] The Wellbeing Purpose is about creating life-changing opportunities in the supply chain for those who value them the most. To learn more about the benefits of wellbeing for employees, we must continue our journey across the footprint of business. We must leave the supply chain and arrive at the busy manufacturing facilities, offices and shops that are owned and controlled by a Wellthy Company. It is here, peeking into the lives of employees, that we'll discover the phenomenally potent case for improving life satisfaction in the workplace.

Notes

1 Smith, A. (1776). *An Inquiry into the Nature and Causes of the Wealth of Nations*. London: Methuen.

2 The story of Tian Yu is detailed in Chan, J. (2013). A suicide survivor: the life of a Chinese worker. *New Technology, Work and Employment*, *28*(2), 84–99. See also Chakrabortty, A. (2013) The woman who nearly died making your iPad. *The Guardian*. Retrieved 1 April 2016, from www.theguardian.com/commentisfree/2013/aug/05/woman-nearly-died-making-ipad.

3 Chan, J. (2013). A suicide survivor: the life of a Chinese worker. *New Technology, Work and Employment*, *28*(2), 84–99.

4 Gallup (2014). *World Faces Shortage in Purpose Wellbeing*. Retrieved 1 April 2016, from www.gallup.com/poll/177191/world-faces-shortage-purpose.aspx.

5 Short, J. L., Toffel, M. W. & Hugill, A. R. (2016). Monitoring global supply chains. *Strategic Management Journal*, *37*, 1878–1897.

6 ActionAid (2010). *ActionAid Brings Its Campaign to the Streets of Leeds and London*. Retrieved 1 April 2016, from www.actionaid.org.uk/news-and-views/asda-campaign-comes-to-leeds-and-london.

7 London SE1 (2010). *Protest over Asian Factory Pay at ASDA in Old Kent Road*. Retrieved 1 April 2016, from www.london-se1.co.uk/news/view/4711.

8 Chambers, R. (1995). Poverty and livelihoods: whose reality counts? *Environment and Urbanization*, *7*(1), 173–204.

9 Based on research from Dedehouanou, S. & Maertens, M. (2011). Participation in modern agri-food supply chain in Senegal and happiness. *No. 114447, 2011 International Congress*, 30 August–2 September 2011, Zurich, Switzerland. Zurich: European Association of Agricultural Economists.

10 Terano, R. & Mohamed, Z. (2013). Quality of life among farmers in selected granary areas in Malaysia. *European Journal of Social Sciences*, *41*(1), 100–110.

11 Markussen, T., Fibæk, M., Tarp, F. & Tuan, N. D. A. (2017). The happy farmer: self-employment and subjective well-being in rural Vietnam. *Journal of Happiness Studies*, 1–24.

12 Miller, A. C., Jack, C. G. & Anderson, D. J. (2014, April). An exploration of the factors influencing well-being of farm and non-farm households. *No. 169732, Annual Conference*, 9–11 April 2014, AgroParisTech, Paris, France. Paris: Agricultural Economics Society.

13 Bernie Sanders on Walmart, comments on *The Ed Show*, MSNBC, 3 August 2013.

14 Maslow, A. H. (1943). A theory of human motivation. *Psychological Review*, *50*(4), 370–396.

15 Camfield, L., Choudhury, K. & Devine, J. (2006). *Relationships, Happiness and Well-Being: Insights from Bangladesh*. Bath: ESRC Research Group on Well Being in Developing Countries.

16 Becchetti, L., Castriota, S. & Solferino, N. (2011). Development projects and life satisfaction: an impact study on fair trade handicraft producers. *Journal of Happiness Studies*, *12*(1), 115–138.

17 There is an active debate among economists as to whether those on minimum wages, such as in America, really are on the poverty line or not. See Palumbo, M. (2015). *Will Raising the Minimum Wage Lift Full Time Workers out of Poverty?* Atlanta, GA: Foundation for Economic Education.

18 Ethical Trading Initiative (2015). *Living Wages in Global Supply Chains*. London: Ethical Trading Initiative.

19 Sen, A. K. (1990). Development as capability expansion. In S. Fukuda-Parr et al. (eds.), *Readings in Human Development*. New Delhi & New York: Oxford University Press.

20 Sen, A. K. (1999). *Development as Freedom*. Oxford: Oxford University Press.

21 Wietzke, F. B. & McLeod, C. (2013). Jobs, wellbeing, and social cohesion: evidence from value and perception surveys. *World Bank Policy Research Working Paper* (6447).

22 Graham, C. (2012). *Happiness around the World: The Paradox of Happy Peasants and Miserable Millionaires*. Oxford: Oxford University Press.

23 Clark, A. E. (1997). Job satisfaction and gender: why are women so happy at work? *Labour Economics*, 4(4), 341–372.

24 Borges, P. & Albright, M. (2007). *Women Empowered: Inspiring Change in the Emerging World*. New York: Rizzoli.

25 Walmart (2017). *Women-Owned Businesses*. Retrieved 3 February 2017, from www.walmart.com/cp/women-owned-businesses/1094926.

26 Graham, C. (2012). *Happiness around the World: The Paradox of Happy Peasants and Miserable Millionaires*. Oxford: Oxford University Press.

27 Luthans, F., Avolio, B. J., Walumbwa, F. O. & Li, W. (2005). The psychological capital of Chinese workers: exploring the relationship with performance. *Management and Organization Review*, 1(2), 249–271.

28 Rainforest Alliance (2016). *Rainforest Alliance Certified Palm Oil*, 6 June. Retrieved 2 February 2017, from www.rainforest-alliance.org/articles/rainforest-alliance-certified-palm-oil.

29 Ministry of Food and Agriculture, Republic of Ghana (n.d.). *Brief on the Oil Palm Sector of Ghana*. Retrieved 2 February 2017, from http://mofa.gov.gh/site/?page_id=8819.

30 Dzokoto, V. A. A. (2012). Ghanaian happiness: global, cultural, and phenomenological perspectives. In H. Selin & G. Davey (eds.), *Happiness across Cultures* (pp. 311–327). Dordrecht: Springer.

31 Väth, S. & Gobien, S. (2014). *Life Satisfaction, Contract Farming and Property Rights: Evidence from Ghana*. Joint Discussion Paper Series in Economics (No. 15-2014).

32 Wilshaw, R. (2010). Better jobs in better supply chains. *Oxfam Policy and Practice: Private Sector*, 7(1), 1–20.

33 Ibid.

34 Clean Clothes Campaign (2013). *Rana Plaza: A Man-Made Disaster That Shook the World*. Amsterdam: Clean Clothes Campaign.

35 Markussen, T., Fibæk, M., Tarp, F. & Tuan, N. D. A. (2017). The happy farmer: self-employment and subjective well-being in rural Vietnam. *Journal of Happiness Studies*, 1–24.

36 Becchetti, L., Castriota, S. & Solferino, N. (2011). Development projects and life satisfaction: an impact study on fair trade handicraft producers. *Journal of Happiness Studies*, 12(1), 115–138.

37 Dedehouanou, S. & Maertens, M. (2011). Participation in modern agri-food supply chain in Senegal and happiness. *No. 114447, 2011 International Congress*, 30 August–2 September 2011, Zurich, Switzerland. Zurich: European Association of Agricultural Economists.

38 Blattman, C. & Dercon, S. (2012). *More Sweatshops for Africa? Pilot Results from an Experimental Study of Industrial Labor in Ethiopia*. IGC Working Paper.

39 Blattman, C. & Dercon, S. (2015). *More Sweatshops for Africa? A Randomized Trial of Industrial Jobs and Self-Employment*. Mimeo.

40 Graham, C. (2005). Insights on development from the economics of happiness. *The World Bank Research Observer, 20*(2), 201–231.

41 Pofeldt, E. (2016) The gig economy happiness gap. *Forbes*, 13 February, citing research by Steve King from Emergent Research.

42 Schanberg, S. H. (1996). Six cents an hour. *Life, 19*(7), 38–46.

43 Cushman, J. H. (1998). Nike pledges to end child labor and apply U.S. rules abroad. *New York Times*, 13 May.

44 Peters, C. (2008). The rise of the corporate citizen: Nike's evolving supply chain. *The Chazen Web Journal of International Business*. Retrieved 9 June 2018, from www8.gsb.columbia.edu/researcharchive/articles/3147.

45 Layard, R. (2011). *Happiness: Lessons from a New Science*. London: Penguin. Lord Layard cites the *Journal of Bhutan Studies* for this story.

46 Carrington, K. & McIntosh, A. (2013). *A Literature Review of Wellness, Wellbeing and Quality of Life Issues as They Impact Upon the Australian Mining Sector*. Brisbane: Crime and Justice Research Centre.

47 Fischer, E. F. (2014). *The Good Life: Aspiration, Dignity, and the Anthropology of Wellbeing*. Stanford, CA: Stanford University Press.

48 Ruggie, J. (2008). Protect, respect and remedy: a framework for business and human rights. *Innovations, 3*(2), 189–212.

49 Mondelez International (n.d.). *Coffee Made Happy: Key Facts and Figures*. Retrieved 3 February 2017, from www.mondelezinternational.com/~/media/Mondelez Corporate/uploads/downloads/CoffeeMadeHappyFactsheet.pdf.

50 Mortlock, B. & Hunt, L. M. (2008). *Linking Farmer Wellbeing and Environmentally Sustainable Land Use: A Comparison between Converting Organic and Conventional Dairy Farmers*. Christchurch: ARGOS.

51 Welsch, H. (2002). Preferences over prosperity and pollution: environmental valuation based on happiness surveys. *Kyklos, 55*(4), 473–494; Welsch, H. (2006). Environment and happiness: valuation of air pollution using life satisfaction data. *Ecological Economics, 58*(4), 801–813.

52 Kinver, M. (2015). Aquariums "deliver significant health benefits." *BBC News*, 30 July. Retrieved 3 February 2017, from www.bbc.co.uk/news/science-environment-33716589.

53 Rojas, M. (2007). The complexity of well-being: a life-satisfaction conception and a domains-of-life approach. In I. Gough & A. McGregor (eds.), *Well-Being in Developing Countries: From Theory to Research* (pp. 242–258). New York: Cambridge University Press.

54 Thin, N. (2012). *Social Happiness: Theory into Policy and Practice*. Bristol: Policy Press.

Chapter 5

Make
Employees and the workplace

I know what happiness is, for I have done good work.
Robert Louis Stevenson (1850–1894)[1]

In the late 1920s, at a Western Electric factory outside Chicago, an extraordinary experiment was under way. A sociologist named Elton Mayo was tinkering around with the working conditions. He wanted to find out what affected productivity and wellbeing at work. He adjusted the lighting. He changed the number of breaks. He even brought in hot meals at different times.

A team of friendly researchers noted down any changes to the behaviours of the women selected for the "test room." They informed the participants about the upcoming alterations. They inquired how they felt afterwards. They asked them what made them happy at work and in life.

The early results puzzled Mayo. Despite all the variations, there were few clear patterns to the changes in performance. When the lighting was improved, productivity went up. When he dimmed it again, efficiency still rose. Finally, he returned the factory to its original condition. He increased the hours. He removed rest breaks. He took away the free meals and sent them all in on Saturdays too. Productivity went through the roof.

Mayo was baffled. What was going on? His team reviewed their interviews and drew a conclusion that has had profound implications for workplace wellbeing ever since. The employees put it quite simply: they felt better about their jobs because someone had shown an interest. The researchers had built a strong rapport with the test subjects. They'd asked questions, shown genuine concern for their welfare, warned them in advance about the changes, then asked for feedback on the experiment. As a result, the factory women had become a tightly knit team. They felt a degree of autonomy and rapport that had never existed before. For the first time in their working careers, they felt like they actually mattered.[2]

Elton Mayo's experiments illustrate how human relationships are so fundamental to happiness. In the workplace, how well we get along with colleagues – and customers, suppliers and anyone else – has a huge emotional effect. The women working at the Western Electric factory improved their performance because someone, for the first time, had paid attention to their welfare. The "Hawthorne effect," named after the factory, is the term now used to describe how individuals change their behaviours in response to an awareness of being observed.

Imagine a job where every new starter is given an individual mentor. There is personalized training with regular feedback. A shared vision and core values are instilled right from the start. Sounds pioneering, doesn't it? This is how the ancient Greeks skilled their young soldiers. The idea of mentoring goes back even further to ancient Africa, where kids were assigned a non-family member for learning and development. Likewise, more than 2,500 years ago, China had some of the most rigorous processes for recruiting and motivating high performers. Public administration relied upon it. Experts in people management have been pondering for a very long time how to improve workplace performance.

Countless books have been written on how to nurture efficiency and job satisfaction. Since Mayo's experiments in Chicago, numerous studies have uncovered consistent findings. Job satisfaction blossoms when companies set clear performance goals, give regular feedback, provide a supportive boss, ensure good relationships with colleagues, and provide fair rewards. You can pick up countless HR manuals and wellness case studies that preach the same core tenets.[3]

Yet these steps aren't enough to create a good life. Plenty of people are satisfied at work ("engaged," in the jargon) but still lead a sad existence. Business affects happiness beyond the office walls and factory gates. If we want corporations to play a truly positive role in the world, we need to start thinking about how employment practices affect happiness in the round. This chapter sets out what companies can do in the workplace to raise not just job satisfaction, but life satisfaction.

The job and life satisfaction

This isn't a book about occupational wellbeing. If companies are judged on that record alone, the scoresheet is a bad one. Despite all the HR expertise accumulated over the centuries, most Americans say that they feel unsatisfied at work.[4] In this sense, most businesses are a direct drain on wellbeing.

Job and life satisfaction are quite different. The first concerns our feelings towards, and commitment to, our employer. Job satisfaction is about being content in the workplace, with our occupation and career outlook. But that's just one building block of life. The other domains we looked at in Chapter 2 include our health, personal relationships, financial situation and leisure time. Don't forget: it's perfectly possible to be engaged at work and miserable in our free time, or disengaged at work but delighted with our health, family and friendships.

There is often a strong link between employment and life satisfaction because work is a big part of most people's lives.[5] The average working person spends the majority of their waking hours on the job. The effects, both good and bad, spill over into how we feel about life. Fulfilling work and great workmates can last beyond the 9 to 5. Equally, stress, indignity and exposure to dangerous conditions may be felt after the production line has ceased for the day. Working patterns affect our health, how much free time we have, and our relationships at home.

These linkages matter for business because the benefits flow both ways. Happiness at work can contribute to contentment with life. And those more satisfied with life are most likely to be satisfied with their jobs.[6] A Wellthy Company benefits when employees feel good about life because they put more into – and get more out of – their occupation.

The real value of work is that a job can provide a sense of meaning. From the accountant to the zoologist, many people define themselves by their profession. It can provide a sense of identity, a personal purpose that motivates and inspires.

Although this chapter is called "Make," fewer and fewer people in the West manufacture goods anymore. One in nine jobs in America is now in retail.[7] But every job creates something. A shop or call centre creates an experience; a marketing campaign delivers new ideas. It is the process of making that provides the meaning to work. The best way for business to create meaning is not just to focus on the tasks at hand, the making and selling of products and services. It's to ask employees to play a part in something bigger.

Labour's role in life

Ever since the 1920s, there's been an idea called the happy-productive worker thesis.[8] This says that happier staff are great to have because they are more productive and less likely to leave. The irony is that although this theory has been around for nearly 100 years, dissatisfaction with work has increased. Meanwhile, many economies face a massive productivity challenge.

Modernization in the workplace has brought more standardization and control. Sure, productivity initially rose sharply in some industries, often supported by new technologies. But neither satisfaction with work nor life has risen with all this so-called progress. When did work become so meaningless and unfulfilling?

In pre-modern times, labour involved a deeply personal relationship with the land. Hunter-gatherers would not recognize the modern idea of "work," spending some days in the thrill of the hunt, and others resting and socializing, according to anthropologists.[9] Life may have been brutish and short, but it seems to have been rarely the labour itself that caused the stress.

The dotted farms of settled agriculture marked an era of challenging endeavour. Working hours increased;[10] famines and epidemics wrought havoc. But in free societies, farming was quite autonomous. Many agricultural labourers would experience varied tasks over the course of a year. Farming was incredibly tough but engaging work.

It was the dawn of the Industrial Revolution that brought our modern mantras of standardization and specialization. Mass production required workflow planning, quality control and a hierarchy to manage the masses. Monitoring and evaluation enabled the bosses to constantly keep track of performance – and micromanage the staff. The result is a world today of jobs with minimal autonomy and maximum oversight.

Our modern ways of working have wrought some calamitous effects on wellbeing. We have no real way of knowing how hunter-gatherers or medieval farmers would have rated their job and life satisfaction. If the studies from the developing world today (which we looked at in Chapters 3 and 4) are anything to go by, the answer might have been "good" to "great" in years when food was bountiful and war and disease kept in check.

The results since the industrial era have been truly shocking. By the mid-1990s, three-quarters of American workers reported high levels of stress on a weekly basis. Around 12 million Britons say that they are bad-tempered and irritable at home as a result of their jobs.[11] An astonishing 7 out of every 10 American workers are not engaged, or are actively disengaged, at work. According to Gallup, this costs the US economy a massive $500 billion in lost productivity every year.[12]

In one area in particular, we are witnessing an epidemic: mental distress. High-pressured work, particularly when coupled with a feeling of powerlessness, accentuates and perpetuates psychological strain.[13] One of the most shocking facts produced by the World Health Organization is that depression is now the leading cause of ill health and disability worldwide.[14] High workloads and long workdays are one of the main reasons for stress, frequently spilling over into conflict and unhappiness at home. Despite the opportunities for new relationships and meaning from modern work, the experience for millions appears to be far from a happy one.

Top companies compete for new recruits with claims to have the happiest workforces. But how many firms can genuinely say they are making life feel better – in the round – for their employees? Hardly any. Most fail to create even basic levels of job satisfaction, let alone life enhancement. To describe this as a missed opportunity is a gross understatement. We have a crisis on our hands. We need to tear up the work plan and ditch the old manuals. We need a drastic and urgent reappraisal of what work is for. The good news for business is that there's a massive prize to be had. Let's start by unpacking that benefit, then see how companies can boost happiness for employees not just with work, but life overall.

Productivity and profitability

There are billions of dollars to be made from improving wellbeing in the workplace. Happier employees make for a more profitable business. The research that's been done on this is truly eye-popping in its conclusions.

Let's start with something as simple as laughter. Students shown comedy clips before sitting a maths exam have been shown to perform significantly better than those who didn't get to chuckle beforehand.[15] In the workplace, employees in a positive mood are between 10% and 12% more productive than other colleagues.[16] That's a dramatic improvement in output from immediate, positive moods.

Are happier employees really better workers? The unequivocal answer is yes. In their book *Happiness at Work*, Jessica Pryce-Jones and colleagues worked out that the most content workers are nearly 50% more productive than the least happy. They take 75% fewer sick days and report twice as much engagement with the business. Most significantly, their satisfaction with life is a whopping 180% higher.[17]

Companies that invest in improving the wellbeing of the workforce can reap a double dividend: higher productivity and profits, and a bigger impact on society through greater life satisfaction. It's a self-supporting circle of happier employees who work harder, put more into the job and get more out of life.

But hold on a second. Aren't these happier people to begin with? You might think that successful businesses are just cherry-picking the more optimistic recruits. Could that explain their outperformance? That's partially true. In a competitive market for talent, you can select staff who are more predisposed to happiness as one route to improved performance. But just as we saw in Chapter 4 with the supply chain, sometimes picking employees with lower wellbeing and giving them a great opportunity can have a disproportionate impact on life. The effects will be felt more sharply. So, it's not simply a matter of recruiting happier people. Unhappier people given life-changing opportunities can turbocharge productivity too.

Employee retention is a significant challenge for many firms. Skilled labour and experienced staff can be costly to replace. Research shows that the happiest employees are by far the most loyal. Those who rate their satisfaction with life the highest are most likely to be committed to their organization, more satisfied with their careers and less likely to leave.[18]

One massive study of 9,000 people from across the world found that employees who reported being happiest at work stayed twice as long in their jobs, took 10 times less sick leave, and spent twice as much time focused on their jobs compared to the least happy.[19] Because staff turnover can be significantly reduced through enhancing wellbeing, a direct link to higher profitability can follow.[20]

One term, around 400 students at Carnegie Mellon University in Pittsburgh were given a nasal spray that exposed them to a cold virus. Students who reported higher levels of stress and unhappiness were more than three times as likely to catch the cold.[21] This illustrates how happier people are more resilient and less likely to be sick, depressed or otherwise absent from work.[22] Happier workers even have better safety records.[23]

Other studies have shown that positive, hopeful people can endure pain for up to twice as long as others. Most companies aren't in the business of intentionally creating pain for their employees. But the research suggests that those with a positive mindset perform better in challenging situations, a "happiness advantage" amid the daily trials of many workplaces.[24]

It's rare to find a business today that doesn't have "innovation" or "creativity" plastered on the walls. These are some of the most common corporate values. But how many firms invest in wellbeing as a route to creativity? Happier people are likely to be much more innovative. Those put in a good mood tend to be more original, creative and flexible in their thinking.[25] Wellbeing has also been linked to more cooperative and collaborative behaviours – essential skills in most modern work environments.[26]

Higher productivity. More resilience and less absence. Greater creativity. All these can reduce costs and help the bottom line. But the biggest benefit by far comes to the top line: rising sales. Just think about it from the customer's perspective. Who would you rather do business with: a firm of averagely content staff or a business brimming with optimism and infectious warmth?

Superb customer relationships are without doubt the biggest benefit from staff wellbeing. Study after study has found that happier employees are far better at customer relations. This is particularly important for front-line jobs such as retail where interpersonal skills support sales. Shoppers dealing with positive, satisfied staff will come back time and again. This is the reason why, when the calculations have been done, happier workforces have been shown to create higher profits and better returns for shareholders.[27]

It's important to reiterate that we are not just talking about short-term moods. Smiles from a salesperson that disappear when you turn your back are neither effective nor sustainable. Instead, a Wellthy Company aspires for staff to feel better about life. That doesn't mean permanent grinning. But it does mean more resilient, confident, focused, loyal and productive employees.

Happier staff make more sales, drive bigger revenues and ultimately increase profits. This means two things for companies. First, firms should recruit with wellbeing in mind. That doesn't always mean recruiting the most optimistic people. It requires considering the potential for raising wellbeing when hiring staff. Businesses should ensure the recruitment pool includes those out-of-work, marginalised groups and other less content communities.

Second, all organizations should invest in improving happiness in the workplace. It's a no-brainer to create those positive moods, job satisfaction, corporate engagement and all the things that make people love going to work. But that's not enough. To really harness the commercial and social value of a happier workforce, business needs to start thinking big. Our purpose is for all staff to lead more satisfied and fulfilling lives.

Purpose in the workplace

Organizations thrive when they share a common focus. Having a vision and goals creates a collective aim for companies as well as the individuals that work in them. Academics have shown that when staff understand what the business is striving to achieve, and feel like they can contribute to it, happiness soars.[28] But it's not just any old corporate ambition. Earnings per share simply isn't enough. The corporate mission must mean something. The Wellbeing Purpose is about organizing, mobilizing and inspiring by taking a stand on something that benefits society and enhances life.

A social purpose explains *why* an organization exists. It sets out an ambition beyond the commercial priorities or the traditional corporate mission. It articulates the value that the business wants to create for the world. The premise of this book is that societal wellbeing should be the ultimate purpose of all responsible businesses. But each company will want to craft its own edge to this challenge. Pharmaceutical and food companies could focus on health; technology and transport might fortify relationships. Each corporation should pick a cause that is relevant but underpinned by the science of life satisfaction.

A great purpose with a social edge provides the passion and motivation to get more out of work. It can help staff to feel part of something bigger, to provide for that yearning to contribute to a greater good. Rising rates of depression in the West have been attributed to a loss of meaning. Perhaps that's because fewer people have a god or close-knit social club nowadays.

To rediscover meaning, we need to be attached to something larger than ourselves – what self-help expert Martin Seligman has described as a calling for a greater good.[29] Business can help. Of course, companies can't fill this void completely. But firms with an essence of social value can make working feel worthwhile. Why does the business exist? What benefit does it bring to the world? Among potential employees, particularly from millennials and Generation Y, "having a job where I can make an impact" on the world is a more important driver of happiness than money or having a prestigious career.[30]

Research suggests that companies that craft a clear social ambition have happier, more engaged and more effective workforces.[31] How meaningful someone perceives their work to be is one of the biggest influences on how satisfied they feel about life.[32]

In order to provide real worth, the purpose must be genuine. Employees will see through the spin if it's simply a strapline to a short-lived campaign. A social purpose needs to be baked into the business and integrated into the products and services. It must actively shape the daily decisions that staff and management make.

Goals also matter for individuals. For any employee, personal objectives need to be just that right level of stretch: too demanding, and they demotivate; too timid, and they lack bite. Inspiring goals can create a much happier workforce, particularly when coupled with feedback that instils a sense of accomplishment.[33] There must be a careful alignment between personal goals and the company-wide social purpose. By setting individual goals that support a wider ambition, business can create meaning and inspire a more committed, motivated and happier workplace.

Employees work harder, perform better and feel happier when they have tasks that are meaningful and morally worthwhile.[34] Research even suggests that just working in an ethical environment can raise job satisfaction if the values are put into practice.[35] This is because the happiest individuals tend to have spiritual and philosophical beliefs that are reflected in their daily lives.[36]

Flow

There is a popular video you can watch online called the Gorilla Experiment.[37] The viewer's task is to count the number of passes of a ball that is thrown between players. What most people don't notice is that halfway through, a guy dressed as a gorilla runs into the middle of the game and gesticulates comically at the camera. When told to focus on counting the number of passes, half of Harvard students fail to notice the gorilla. When you play it back, it seems astonishing – even hilarious – that anyone could miss this massive animal aping about.

In their book *The Gorilla Experiment*, Christopher Chabris and Daniel Simons describe how we can become so absorbed and focused on a task that we lose sight of everything else around us. Michael Jackson used to tell a story of how, being driven down a freeway in his Rolls Royce, he was so ensconced in his test tape of "Billie Jean" that he failed to notice that his car engine had caught fire.[38]

Focus and absorption are great for wellbeing. Although some people like to have a moan about boring tasks at work, it's pressure, stress and poor relationships that frustrate the most. From the farmer toiling a field to the consultant populating a spreadsheet, even mundane tasks can be highly engaging. When absolutely immersed in a challenging activity that stretches us, most people get a surprising amount out of it.

In his seminal book from 1990, the Hungarian psychologist Mihaly Csikszentmihalyi called this flow.[39] Flow is a state of intense concentration. By channelling our focus on a task, we enter a state of total immersion. We use the expression "in the zone" to describe that feeling when we are so absorbed that we fail to notice distractions. The task becomes automatic. We lose an awareness of our own consciousness. Time seems to fly by.

Csikszentmihalyi undertook some studies revealing just how beneficial flow is for wellbeing. Participants given electronic beepers were asked to periodically rate their happiness. What he discovered has intriguing implications for workplaces and life. Rather than mindless wandering – daydreaming about whatever we like – most happiness comes from focused engagement on a single activity.

Flow is much more than an absence of distraction. It is a state of active concentration and stimulation. Subsequent research has shown that flow is not just great for momentary moods; it boosts life satisfaction too.[40]

A Wellthy Company raises both occupational and life satisfaction by structuring work to increase flow. This needn't be limited to professional, white-collar jobs that require a heavy dose of thinking. Opportunities to flow can be built into activities from preparing food to stocking a shop – in fact, any activity where you apply skills in focused concentration.

The task needs to be stimulating and challenging. Csikszentmihalyi insists on the point that skills combined with challenge are the key to flow. But there is one final element that's vital for flow: control. If a staff member can't decide for themselves whether to start or stop an activity, or switch from one project to another, they cannot flow. Put more simply, flow is impossible without freedom.

Freedoms at work

Of all the possible ways that an organization affects happiness, one topic keeps coming up time and time again. How much control we have over what we do each day has a monumental effect. Aristotle believed that women, slaves, merchants and farmers could not achieve true happiness (what he called *eudaemonia*) because they lacked freedom. If you can't make your own decisions, you can't make the choices that lead to happiness.

The Wellbeing Purpose involves three freedoms in the workplace. The first is freedom from unnecessary interruptions. In most offices, phones ringing and other colleagues chatting are major causes of distraction. People spend an average of just two to three minutes focused on a task before switching. Once interrupted, it typically takes 25 minutes to return to a project.[41]

We compensate for interruptions by working faster, experiencing more frustration and more stress.[42] Workplaces must be liberated from interruptions. We need more quiet spaces and room for focused concentration. Positive relationships and time to relax and laugh are vital, but they mustn't be at the expense of space to escape. That's the first step to helping more people to reach that point of absorption and delight.

The second essential freedom is from micromanagement. In general, more autonomy leads to more happiness. Each employee needs a level of independence to decide how to structure their day, performing tasks in an order they choose, starting some and stopping others at different times. Independent working can be a major boost to wellbeing. That's easier in a shop or office job than a factory production line, but any job can be designed to enable some choice.

Autonomy creates the opportunity for another crucial component: variety. Variety provides stimulation, helping to retain attention and increase motivation. Jobs that combine autonomy with variety are consistently ranked highest for job satisfaction.[43] Independence at work and variety during the day are, in turn, powerful predictors of life satisfaction.[44]

There is a convincing business case for these two freedoms: autonomy and variety can raise productivity and creativity. Studies show that when people have more control over their tasks, they are motivated to work at them for longer.[45] Innovation flourishes with empowerment. There is a famous story of how Art Fry used his "permitted bootlegging" time at 3M in the early 1970s to develop an adhesive bookmark for his hymn book. It became the world-famous Post-it note. Google used to encourage staff to spend up to 20% of their time on special projects. This freedom came up with Gmail, AdSense and Google News – each massive commercial successes for the company.[46]

Freedom to experiment, tinker and vary what we do matters for individuals and companies. Autonomy has such a powerful effect on happiness that the writer Robert Frank has suggested that employees should demand more freedom to use different skills – or change their office set-up – in exchange for a lower salary.[47] If management at most large companies proposed such a pay cut, there would no doubt be howls of protest from staff and unions alike. But it's worth thinking about this for a moment. What the research suggests is that freedom at work matters so much more than small differences in wages. There seems to be something hardwired into humans about choice. This may explain why democratic freedoms show such a strong connection to wellbeing across societies.[48] We want a say in determining our own day as well as who rules us. At work, given the choice between better pay or more independence and choice, most people would be wise to put freedom first.

Freedom from interruptions and micromanagement are all part of a healthy work environment. Before we look at one final freedom, it's worth summarizing what decades of research shows about how to turbocharge happiness in places of work. This is absolutely not about jolly offices with funky table tennis tables and free beer. Health and relationships affect life satisfaction more than anything else. A quick game of ping-pong or "happy hour" drinks really only matter as far as they improve relationships with colleagues.

What can a Wellthy Company substantively do to maximize long-term happiness in the workplace? For health, we need more businesses to provide a culture and infrastructure to integrate healthy eating and regular exercise into the daily routine.[49] Good food, free healthcare, cycle-to-work schemes and subsidized gym memberships are only the start. More substantively, what about regular lifestyle assessments, proactive screening for common health conditions and time off for preventative (not just reactive) check-ups? Mental health issues need to be taken as seriously as physical impediments. If we know that health matters massively for wellbeing, companies need to think strategically about how they can help staff to live longer, healthier, more fulfilling lives.

Relationships at work need to be purposefully nurtured. That's exactly what Elton Mayo accidentally discovered at the Hawthorne factory in the 1920s. The work environment mattered, but not nearly as much as how well the women got on with each other and the research team. An effective line manager is important: supervisors who communicate openly and clearly create happier workplaces.[50] But relationships with co-workers matter more than how well people get on with the boss.[51] Friendly colleagues that gel as teams have a remarkably powerful association with wellbeing.[52]

When a firm is tempted to renovate the office or upgrade the factory, it will no doubt provide a brilliant emotional boost. But the real prize stems from a laser-like focus on health, the quality of relationships, job security and recognition, and rewards that are seen as fair.

It's not just relationships at work that are affected by companies. Relationships at home matter just as much, if not more. But when did you last hear a company say they wanted to strengthen marriages, celebrate families or enable stronger friendships outside of work? These are the crucial ingredients to a happy life. A Wellthy Company supports relationships through one final liberty: freedom *from* work.

Freedom from work

In 1930, John Maynard Keynes made a bold prediction. Within 100 years, he forecast, we'd all be working just 15 hours a week.[53] We've not got many years to go, but it looks like his prediction will be wide of the mark (global rates vary, but the average today is around 40 hours).

Keynes made a plausible assumption. He reasoned that advances in technology and productivity would mean that we wouldn't need to put in the same hours each day to attain the same standard of living. The problem is that while living standards have risen, so have the opportunities to work more, buy a bigger house, take on more debt and spend more on holidays and cars. We carry on working to service the twenty-first century's hyper-consuming, hyper-working lifestyle.

Today, many people, particularly in wealthier countries, find themselves relatively rich in material things, but poor in something else: time. We'll look at the pluses and perils of materialism in the next chapter. But what really affects wellbeing is not material affluence. It's something called time affluence.[54]

The solution stretches beyond the obvious: flexible working and better work–life balance. To really improve wellbeing, we need more companies to give staff back that precious resource of time.

Time is a funny thing when it comes to work and wellbeing. Too many free hours, and those who are underemployed feel dissatisfied. Increased demand for labour seems to improve happiness up to around 35 to 55 hours per week, depending on the culture and individual.[55] Despite Keynes' vision, we've created societies where labour matters just as much as leisure to our identities and feelings of self-worth. But beyond this threshold, the hours become corrosive. They eat into the rest of life. People stop working in order to live, and begin living in order to work. If the patterns of work are onerous and regimented, they scar particularly deeply. For example, the inflexibility of shift work has been shown to cause particular conflict at home, as well as physical and mental health problems.[56]

Business erodes wellbeing when it fails to facilitate choices. A poor work–life balance is one of the greatest predictors of stress.[57] Each individual should be able to reach their own ideal in terms of time at work and be paid in proportion to that choice.

Discretionary time is the term used to describe the number of hours that an individual controls in their day. There is an incredibly strong link between how much discretionary time someone has and how satisfied they rate their life.[58] From spending time with loved ones to absorption in hobbies, leisure time ranks across all cultures as a major determinant of happiness. This is why flexible working comes up time and again as vital to job satisfaction. By enabling choice, agile working also has dramatic impacts on satisfaction with life. Freedom enables each individual to make choices about how to pass their hours.

A Wellthy Company frees up more free time. The options are plentiful: flexible start and finish times, homeworking, job-sharing, part-time working, career breaks, compressed hours, weekend working, term-time working, unpaid leave. You may think that it's not possible for many businesses to provide such choices. But it's fast becoming the norm, and a legal requirement in some countries, to consider requests for flexibility. Increasingly, all businesses are realizing that flexible options are not just possible, but desirable, as they typically boost productivity and happiness.

Perhaps the demand isn't there? Given the choice, would most people choose to work reduced hours? Consider a study that found that around two-thirds of American adults feel too much pressure to work. Over half say they would be willing to forego a full day's pay in order to regularly work a four-day week.[59]

There may be a difference between what people tell a survey they are willing to do and actually follow through with. Cultural acceptance plays a role here. But business can facilitate these choices. There are signs of change afoot. In the UK, the law changed in 2014, and now anyone employed for more than six months has a right to request flexible working. The US, which long lagged the world on paid parental leave, now has state-run family leave systems in California, New Jersey and Rhode Island.[60]

Seismic shifts in gender roles and family life are driving the need for increased flexibility. One hundred years ago, women made up less than 20% of the American workforce. Today, it's nearly half. More women are working and doing so for longer hours. Surveys suggest that many women (though by no means all) are happiest when given the opportunity to work part-time.[61] Meanwhile, more men are helping out at home. Since the 1960s, American dads have more than doubled the time spent doing household chores and nearly tripled their time spent on childcare.[62] Yet fathers opting to take shared parental leave is as low as 2% in the UK. The lack of awareness and cultural stereotypes are both something that businesses must help to address.[63]

When it comes to happiness, we know that whether someone has supportive, strong relationships at home is one of the most powerful predictors of life satisfaction. Work–family conflict cuts into wellbeing. It's not just young families. An ageing workforce in many Western economies has created a "sandwich generation" with growing responsibilities to help care for elderly relatives. In order to boost our world's wellbeing, we need more companies to ask whether their working practices are helping to promote strong families and loving relationships.

Finally, there is one time of the day that absolutely wrecks wellbeing: the dreaded commute. That won't surprise those readers with a tedious journey. Research suggests that a long trip to work causes a dramatic cut to life satisfaction. What's surprising is that so few people accurately factor this in to decisions about where to live and what job to take. We are amazingly bad at forecasting the expected benefits from a bigger house or a higher salary when it means a longer trip to the office. One study from Germany found that a commute of just 22 minutes requires a 19% higher salary to compensate.[64] While companies can't control where staff choose to live, they can provide options – from remote working to flexible start and finish times – that make commuting more bearable.

To summarize, staff need to be clear on their goals, rooted in a wider social purpose. Freedom from interruptions and micromanagement provide the autonomy, variety and sense of control needed to flow and get the most out of work. But it's freedom from work that marks a Wellthy Company's single greatest contribution to employee happiness. We've seen in previous chapters how employment opportunities and job security typically matter much more than pay levels. A reliable, stable job that excites and engages needs to be coupled with ample time to experience life beyond the workplace.

Companies should measure life satisfaction for all employees and track progress on a regular basis. This is not the standard question on how "engaged" people feel with the corporate body. That's way too narrow. What we really want to know is whether business is doing anything to help staff feel better about life. Why don't companies ask the question: how satisfied are you with life, and what can your employer do to help your existence have more enjoyment and meaning?

We need firms to act as a responsible employer, embracing the long-term interests of staff. Pensions saving is a great example. Studies indicate that most people are happy to be enrolled in schemes, but often don't get around to doing so (hence why the British government has made auto-enrolment the default). Encouraging the long-term financial wellbeing of staff can boost happiness in the years beyond work.

All this can be great for productivity and the bottom line. Of course, not all investments in happiness will have a great payback. Reading some of the books on occupational wellbeing, you'd think every business should be pouring millions of dollars into boosting staff conditions, training and perks. This is a false promise. We need to remember the costs.[65] There is clearly a threshold where investment in happiness makes sense. We need many more companies to pioneer fresh approaches to boosting happiness in the round, and measure how life satisfaction loops back to raise motivation, retention and output. That's how to build a business case.

Elton Mayo's experiments at the Hawthorne factory were the first to identify that people perform best when managers focus on relationships. Without doubt, one of the strongest benefits of a happier workforce is more effective personal interactions, particularly with customers. Brilliant customer service flows from a workforce that is motivated and optimistic. This positive approach is the first step in our plan for marketing that enhances life.

Notes and references

1 Cited in Hubbard, E. (1916). *Robert Louis Stevenson and Fanny Osbourne*. New York: Hartford Lunch Company.
2 Mayo, E. (1930). The Hawthorne experiment. *The Human Factor*, 6; Mayo, E. (1949). Hawthorne and the Western Electric Company. *Public Administration: Concepts and Cases*, 149–158.
3 For a good summary, see New Economics Foundation (2014). *Wellbeing at Work: A Review of the Literature*. London: New Economics Foundation.
4 Conference Board (2014). *Job Satisfaction: 2014 Edition*. New York: Conference Board.
5 Judge, T. A. & Watanabe, S. (1993). Another look at the job satisfaction–life satisfaction relationship. *Journal of Applied Psychology*, 78(6), 939–948.
6 Ibid.
7 Thompson, D. (2013). Death of the salesmen: technology's threat to retail jobs. *The Atlantic*, June.
8 Zelenski, J. M., Murphy, S. A. & Jenkins, D. A. (2008). The happy-productive worker thesis revisited. *Journal of Happiness Studies*, 9(4), 521–537.
9 Donkin, R. (2010). *The History of Work*. London: Palgrave Macmillan.
10 Diamond, J. (2012). *The World until Yesterday: What Can We Learn from Traditional Societies?* New York: Penguin.

11 Gavin, J. H. & Mason, R. O. (2004). The virtuous organization: the value of happiness in the workplace. *Organizational Dynamics*, *33*(4), 379–392.

12 Gallup (2013). *State of the American Workplace*. Washington, DC: Gallup.

13 Stansfeld, S. & Candy, B. (2006). Psychosocial work environment and mental health: a meta-analytic review. *Scandinavian Journal of Work, Environment & Health*, *32*(6), 443–462.

14 World Health Organization (2017). *"Depression: Let's Talk" Says WHO, as Depression Tops List of Causes of Ill Health*. Geneva: World Health Organization.

15 Oswald, A. J., Proto, E. & Sgroi, D. (2015). Happiness and productivity. *Journal of Labor Economics*, *33*(4), 789–822.

16 Ibid.

17 Pryce-Jones, J. (2011). *Happiness at Work: Maximizing Your Psychological Capital for Success*. New York: John Wiley & Sons.

18 Harter, J. K., Schmidt, F. L. & Hayes, T. L. (2002). Business-unit-level relationship between employee satisfaction, employee engagement, and business outcomes: a meta-analysis. *Journal of Applied Psychology*, *87*(2), 268–279; De Neve, J. E., Diener, E., Tay, L. & Xuereb, C. (2013). The objective benefits of subjective well-being. In J. Helliwell, R. Layard & J. Sachs (eds.), *World Happiness Report 2013* (pp. 54–79). New York: UN Sustainable Development Solutions Network.

19 Pryce-Jones, J. (2011). *The Five Drivers of Happiness at Work*. Retrieved 25 April 2017, from https://blogs.wsj.com/source/2011/09/18/the-five-drivers-of-happiness-at-work/.

20 Harter, J. K., Schmidt, F. L., Asplund, J. W., Killham, E. A. & Agrawal, S. (2010). Causal impact of employee work perceptions on the bottom line of organizations. *Perspectives on Psychological Science*, *5*(4), 378–389.

21 Cohen, S., Tyrrell, D. A. & Smith, A. P. (1991). Psychological stress and susceptibility to the common cold. *New England Journal of Medicine*, *325*(9), 606–612.

22 Peterson, S. J., Luthans, F., Avolio, B. J., Walumbwa, F. O. & Zhang, Z. (2011). Psychological capital and employee performance: a latent growth modelling approach. *Personnel Psychology*, *64*(2), 427–450.

23 Harter, J. K., Schmidt, F. L. & Hayes, T. L. (2002). Business-unit-level relationship between employee satisfaction, employee engagement, and business outcomes: a meta-analysis. *Journal of Applied Psychology*, *87*(2), 268–279.

24 Achor, S. (2011). *The Happiness Advantage: The Seven Principles of Positive Psychology That Fuel Success and Performance at Work*. London: Virgin Books.

25 New Economics Foundation (2014). *Wellbeing at Work: A Review of the Literature*. London: New Economics Foundation; De Neve, J. E., Diener, E., Tay, L. & Xuereb, C. (2013). The objective benefits of subjective well-being. In J. Helliwell, R. Layard & J. Sachs (eds.), *World Happiness Report 2013* (pp. 54–79). New York: UN Sustainable Development Solutions Network.

26 De Neve, J. E., Diener, E., Tay, L. & Xuereb, C. (2013). The objective benefits of subjective well-being. In J. Helliwell, R. Layard & J. Sachs (eds.), *World Happiness Report 2013* (pp. 54–79). New York: UN Sustainable Development Solutions Network.

27 Robertson, I. & Cooper, C. (2011). *Well-Being: Productivity and Happiness at Work*. Basingstoke: Springer; Harter, J. K., Schmidt, F. L., Asplund, J. W., Killham, E. A. & Agrawal, S. (2010). Causal impact of employee work perceptions on the bottom line of organizations. *Perspectives on Psychological Science*, *5*(4), 378–389.

28 Rato, R. & Davey, G. (2012). Quality of work life in Macau. In H. Selin & G. Davey (eds.), *Happiness across Cultures* (pp. 95–106). Dordrecht: Springer.

29 Seligman, M. E. (2004). *Authentic Happiness: Using the New Positive Psychology to Realize Your Potential for Lasting Fulfillment*. New York: Simon & Schuster.

30 Zukin, C. & Szeltner, M. (2012). *Talent Report: What Workers Want in 2012*. San Francisco, CA: Net Impact.

31 New Economics Foundation (2014). *Wellbeing at Work: A Review of the Literature*. London: New Economics Foundation.

32 Caza, B. & Wrzesniewski, A. (2013). How work shapes well-being. In S. A. David, I. Boniwell & A. C. Ayers (eds.), *The Oxford Handbook of Happiness* (pp. 693–710). Oxford: Oxford Universtiy Press.

33 Diener, E. & Seligman, M. E. (2002). Very happy people. *Psychological Science, 13*(1), 81–84.

34 Ryan, R. M. & Deci, E. L. (2000). Self-determination theory and the facilitation of intrinsic motivation, social development, and well-being. *American Psychologist, 55*(1), 68–78.

35 Peterson, D. K. (2002). Deviant workplace behavior and the organization's ethical climate. *Journal of Business and Psychology, 17*(1), 47–61.

36 Seligman, M. E. (2004). *Authentic Happiness: Using the New Positive Psychology to Realize Your Potential for Lasting Fulfillment*. New York: Simon & Schuster.

37 Simons, D. (2010). *Selective Attention Test*. Retrieved 9 June 2018, from www.youtube.com/watch?v=vJG698U2Mvo; Chabris, C. & Simons, D. (2010). *The Invisible Gorilla: And Other Ways Our Intuitions Deceive Us*. New York: Harmony Books.

38 Jones, L. (2013). 30 cool facts you didn't know about "Billie Jean." *NME*, 2 January.

39 Csikszentmihalyi, M. (1990). *Flow: The Psychology of Optimal Performance*. New York: Cambridge University Press.

40 Collins, A. L., Sarkisian, N. & Winner, E. (2009). Flow and happiness in later life: an investigation into the role of daily and weekly flow experiences. *Journal of Happiness Studies, 10*(6), 703–719.

41 González, V. M. & Mark, G. (2004). Constant, constant, multi-tasking craziness: managing multiple working spheres. In B. Adelson, S. Dumais & J. Olson (eds.), *Proceedings of the SIGCHI Conference on Human Factors in Computing Systems* (pp. 113–120). New York: ACM.

42 Mark, G., Gudith, D. & Klocke, U. (2008, April). The cost of interrupted work: more speed and stress. In B. Adelson, S. Dumais & J. Olson (eds.), *Proceedings of the SIGCHI Conference on Human Factors in Computing Systems* (pp. 107–110). New York: ACM.

43 Fried, Y. (1991). Meta-analytic comparison of the Job Diagnostic Survey and Job Characteristics Inventory as correlates of work satisfaction and performance. *Journal of Applied Psychology, 76*(5), 690–697.

44 Judge, T. A., Locke, E. A., Durham, C. C. & Kluger, A. N. (1998). Dispositional effects on job and life satisfaction: the role of core evaluations. *Journal of Applied Psychology, 83*(1), 17–34.

45 Ryan, R. M. & Deci, E. L. (2000). Self-determination theory and the facilitation of intrinsic motivation, social development, and well-being. *American Psychologist, 55*(1), 68–78.

46 D'Onfro, J. (2015). The truth about Google's "20% time" policy. *Business Insider*, 17 April.

47 Frank, R. H. (1999). *Luxury Fever: Money and Happiness in an Era of Excess*. Princeton, NJ: Princeton University Press.

48 Radcliff, B. (2001). Politics, markets, and life satisfaction: the political economy of human happiness. *American Political Science Review, 95*(4), 939–952.

49 New Economics Foundation (2014). *Wellbeing at Work: A Review of the Literature*. London: New Economics Foundation.

50 Colquitt, J. A., Conlon, D. E., Wesson, M. J., Porter, C. O. & Ng, K. Y. (2001). Justice at the millennium: a meta-analytic review of 25 years of organizational justice research. *Journal of Applied Psychology, 86*(3), 425–445.

51 Erdogan, B., Bauer, T. N., Truxillo, D. M. & Mansfield, L. R. (2012). Whistle while you work: a review of the life satisfaction literature. *Journal of Management, 38*(4), 1038–1083.

52 Humphrey, S. E., Nahrgang, J. D. & Morgeson, F. P. (2007). Integrating motivational, social, and contextual work design features: a meta-analytic summary and theoretical extension of the work design literature. *Journal of Applied Psychology, 92*(5), 1332–1356.

53 Keynes, J. M. (1933). Economic possibilities for our grandchildren. In J. M. Keynes (ed.), *Essays in Persuasion* (pp. 358–373). New York: Harcourt Brace.

54 Kasser, T. (2003). *The High Price of Materialism*. Cambridge, MA: MIT Press.

55 New Economics Foundation (2014). *Wellbeing at Work: A Review of the Literature*. London: New Economics Foundation; Dolan, P., Peasgood, T. & White, M. (2008). Do we really know what makes us happy? A review of the economic literature on the factors associated with subjective well-being. *Journal of Economic Psychology, 29*(1), 94–122.

56 Caza, B. & Wrzesniewski, A. (2013). How work shapes well-being. In S. A. David, I. Boniwell & A. C. Ayers (eds.), *The Oxford Handbook of Happiness* (pp. 693–710). Oxford: Oxford University Press.

57 New Economics Foundation (2014). *Wellbeing at Work: A Review of the Literature*. London: New Economics Foundation.

58 Goodin, R. E., Rice, J. M., Parpo, A. & Eriksson, L. (2008). *Discretionary Time: A New Measure of Freedom*. Cambridge: Cambridge University Press.

59 Kasser, T. & Sheldon, K. M. (2009). Time affluence as a path toward personal happiness and ethical business practice: empirical evidence from four studies. *Journal of Business Ethics, 84*(2), 243–255.

60 At the time of writing, President Trump's proposed 2018 federal budget has outlined a national plan. Lussenhop, J. (2017). Will Trump bring paid maternity leave to the US? *BBC News Online*, 5 May.

61 Warr, P. (2011). *Work, Happiness, and Unhappiness*. New York: Psychology Press.

62 Parker, K. & Livingstone, G. (2016). *Six Facts about American Fathers*. Retrieved 22 May 2017, from www.pewresearch.org/fact-tank/2016/06/16/fathers-day-facts/.

63 BBC News (2018). Shared parental leave take-up may be as low as 2%. *BBC News Online*, 12 February.

64 Stutzer, A. & Frey, B. S. (2008). Stress that doesn't pay: the commuting paradox. *The Scandinavian Journal of Economics, 110*(2), 339–366.

65 Shackleton, J. R. (2012). Wellbeing at work: any lessons? In P. Booth (ed.), . . . *And the Pursuit of Happiness: Wellbeing and the Role of Government*. London: Institute of Economic Affairs, in association with Profile Books.

Chapter 6

Sell

Marketing for life enhancement

> What consumerism really is, at its worst, is getting people to buy things that don't actually improve their lives.
>
> Jeff Bezos, founder of Amazon[1]

Like many parents, Monet Parham finds that her daughters can be quite demanding. "I can tell them 'No' all day long, but then they see commercials that convince them you've really got to have this," the Californian explained. Maya, aged 6, said that buying her favourite food is like getting "a birthday present . . . it's fun and exciting and it surprises me."

The arguments about what meals her girls could have were causing frictions in the family. One heavily marketed product was the cause of so much anguish that the mother took an extraordinary step. She decided to sue the manufacturers for "exploiting children." Monet Parham brought a class action lawsuit against the McDonald's Happy Meal – essentially for making her family unhappy.[2]

The Happy Meal was first introduced in 1979. It's been specifically marketed at children ever since. The box comes with a little toy, and you can pick from a combination of mains, sides and drinks. The format is available right across the world, from "Cajita Feliz" ("Happy Little Box") in Latin America to "Happy Set" in Japan.

Any trip to McDonald's illustrates how the Happy Meal appears to make kids very happy. The figures make the point. McDonald's is the largest toy distributor in the world. It's been rated children's favourite restaurant, with nearly 40% of American kids listing it as their first choice.[3] Hundreds of parents in the UK voted McDonald's the top brand for "pester power." Such phenomenal popularity has helped the business to chalk up $25 billion in revenues a year and open 17 new restaurants every week.[4] It's so successful that the meal-with-toy approach has been copied by many other fast-food chains.

The growth has been powered by aggressive marketing: American children see over 1,000 fast-food commercials on television each year, and hundreds more from McDonald's than any other brand. The marketing has been phenomenally successful: a whopping 96% of American kids can identify the character Ronald McDonald by name – second only to Santa Claus.[5]

McDonald's has been accused of repeatedly and deliberately targeting youngsters early on in life to hook them on its brand.[6] The problem is that this fast food is contributing to startlingly high rates of obesity and diabetes among children. According to the Physicians Committee for Responsible Medicine, a cheeseburger Happy Meal has 520 calories, 20 grams of fat, 8 grams of saturated fat, 50 milligrams of cholesterol and a massive 880 milligrams of sodium. The doctors, who brought the lawsuit with Monet Parham, claimed that "Happy Meals are marketed as explicitly for children, and then children are rewarded with toys for consuming the high amounts of fat and sodium."[7]

All this presents a conundrum. We know that health is one of the three vital ingredients of wellbeing. As we saw in Chapter 2, poor diet is a major cause of deteriorating health that can wreck quality of life and create misery in the years ahead. But kids carry on consuming. Parents carry on buying. How can we explain this contradiction?

Selling happiness

Happiness sells. Coca-Cola promises us that we will "open happiness."[8] Pepsi competes with "the joy of cola." Disney World is the "happiest place on earth." "Your happiness loves Cadbury" tempts us from the chocolate aisle, while "happiness is a quick starting car," according to Esso in the 1950s. Best Buy's trademarked slogan for its gift cards is "No fees. No expiration dates. Just happiness."

When 7-Up was first introduced to China, the parent company PepsiCo considered the literal translation of the brand name: Qi Shang. Unfortunately, this means agitated or disturbed. The phrasing was quickly dismissed as an unsuitable emotion for selling the sugary water. Instead, PepsiCo called the drink Qixi, which means "seven happinesses." The results were incredible. It has been such a successful strapline that the drink is now used as a toast to happiness at Chinese weddings. Who wouldn't want their matrimonial salutation to be to the seven happinesses?[9]

These brands have sought to capitalize on the warm associations between joyful experiences and consuming a product. Most of these products aren't promising happiness in any literal sense – but they have been accused of what the academic Neil Thin has dubbed "corporate happwash." They are selling through a dubious association with wellbeing.[10] The subliminal message is that this brand will bring you a powerful moment of pleasure.

The award for the most telling example of all must go to "happiness is a cigar called Hamlet" – a famous advertising campaign that was run by Hamlet Cigars in the UK until the 1990s. Just like the Happy Meal, marketing cigars as promoting happiness illustrates a striking tension. Many of these products delight us with instant gratification. We carry on buying them. But the very same treats can be devastating for our health and wellbeing if consumed to excess over time.

Snack foods, alcoholic drinks, cigarettes and gambling all demonstrate the tension between short-term kicks and long-term health and happiness. There is genuine enjoyment in the moment. For example, Taiwanese kids that regularly devour fast food and fizzy drinks have been found to be *less* unhappy.[11] Those that don't get a regular dose of unhealthy food are essentially missing out on some "moments of joy."

Neuroscientists have shown that munching on fatty, salty and sugary foods causes our bodies to release endogenous opioids. These create feelings of calmness and satisfaction. They even help to control pain.[12] High-fat, high-calorie foods have been shown to have a similar effect on the brain to taking cocaine and heroin.[13] That's why we carry on buying them.

This addictive kick is what creates the problem. It's because these products are so appealing that they are consumed to excess. Unsurprisingly, those Taiwanese kids that ate more junk food were also more likely to be obese.[14] In the long run, then, they are likely to be unhappier. This craving for consumption is fuelling obesity epidemics, as well as public health crises caused by smoking and gambling.

Is the customer always right?

Adam Smith famously described a hidden hand. By acting in our own self-interest, the free market finds an equilibrium of buyers' needs and sellers' supplies. Economists refer to this as utility maximization. According to the theory, we buy things that we derive a benefit from. So, there is a simple way to determine what makes us happy: look at what we spend our money on. Trillions of choices by billions of consumers every day paint a picture of what really makes life better.

Every purchase meets a need. We buy a hamburger to nourish and enjoy. A car meets a requirement for transport, but also perhaps status and fashion. If something sells, it's because it makes someone happy. After all, wouldn't we just stop buying (or switch brand) if it didn't?

Rational choice theory relies on three assumptions. First, that we know what's best for us. Buying the car will make me feel great and my commute more bearable. Second, that we can accurately weigh up alternatives. It would be better to buy the new car than rent one, use taxis or take the train. Third, that we can accurately forecast our future feelings. I won't regret my choice of transport in a year's time, even when I spot a better model or realize its true running costs.

The idea that the customer is always right assumes that we take in all the available information, weigh up alternatives, judge what's in our best long-term interests and act accordingly. The problem is that huge volumes of research show this to be false.

Shoppers entering one American grocery store were surprised to be met by a lady offering free muffins. Did they bring a grocery list, she asked? What were they planning on buying today? It was all part of a sneaky experiment to see how our appetite affects buying habits. Daniel Gilbert from Harvard University and his colleagues discovered that shoppers who had just eaten a muffin were much more likely to stick to their planned purchases. Hungry shoppers bought more spontaneous items for the week ahead because they falsely assumed that they would be ravenous *for the entire week*.[15]

These errors of logic are called cognitive biases. The "hungry shopper" test shows what's called anchoring: our assumptions about our future feelings are shaped by how we currently feel. We frequently fail to act in our own long-term interests.[16] Typically, most people seek immediate gratification at the expense of benefits further down the line. Short-term consumer borrowing at extortionate rates – frequently regretted[17] – is a case in point.

Nobel Prize-winning economist Daniel Kahneman has popularized the science around heuristics.[18] These are shortcuts that we use to make decisions quickly. They can make our choices appear irrational. Snack foods, slot machines, payday loans and alcohol are just a few examples of products that make consumers act in strange ways.

Millions of smokers continue to buy cigarettes when diagnosed with lung cancer. The British tabloids have described how one Briton, so morbidly obese that he could not get out of bed, continued to feed himself chocolate bars, ice cream and fry-ups – gorging himself on his deathbed.[19]

Our poor forecasting – and lack of self-control – is neatly illustrated by a study of health club memberships in New England. People significantly overpaid for gym memberships up front – even when they could pay on a per use basis. They predicted (or perhaps hoped) that they'd use the gym far more than they did. The researchers found that gym users signed up to "commit" themselves to future exercise but failed to have the self-control to carry through with the plans.[20]

Most people are more impulsive and less rational than traditional economics would have us believe. We are flummoxed by trade-offs and swayed by our circumstances. Above all, we fail to forecast our future feelings, overestimating our future happiness and underestimating how quickly we'll adapt to new purchases.[21]

The customer is not always right. This has huge implications for brands. Most people are overestimating the benefits that will stem from shopping. Consumers end up purchasing much more than their rational self ought to.[22] We are buying stuff that won't satisfy us and paying more for items than we really should.[23]

This is especially true when it comes to impulse purchases. Retailers know this when they tempt us with time-limited sales, one-click online shopping and pumping music in stores. This induces an emotionally "hot" state that drives spontaneous sales. Regret is a common feature of spontaneous shopping. According to one survey, three-quarters of Americans have made an impulse purchase when bored, angry, sad or drunk. Half regretted it – a costly mistake given that 10% spent over $1,000.[24]

Buyer's remorse also extends to big-ticket items. A quarter of Americans say they wouldn't buy their own house again.[25] Yes, you read that right: one in four got it wrong when it came to the biggest purchase of most people's lives! The truth is that many products that are sold every day are not bringing consumers as much joy as they think they will. So, why do we place so much value on things?

Does shopping make us happy?

Materialism's victory is a triumph of marketing. In 1958, the economist J. K. Galbraith kicked off a now familiar debate about wants versus needs. It has dogged the marketing industry ever since. Does marketing satisfy our desires or create unnecessary new ones? For Galbraith, if the company "creates the wants," then it cannot be satisfying genuine need.[26]

Identifying needs that we didn't realize we had is at the core of most consumer marketing. The objective is to entice us, to persuade us that we need that new possession. Emotions are the gateway. Happiness is the promise. But brands must walk a tightrope. They need to create enough enjoyment to generate goodwill – but just enough dissatisfaction to trigger the motivation to buy again.[27]

As Jeff Bezos, founder of Amazon, put it in the quote from 1999 at the start of this chapter, consumerism is often about selling things that *don't* actually improve life.[28] These problems are neatly summarized by Dr Ross McDonald, a psychologist and expert on business ethics:

> The vast majority in society want love, acceptance, respect and esteem from others. They want romance, happiness, success and a sense of positive purpose. And given the fundamental nature of these felt needs . . . people will give inordinate attention to the means by which they might be satisfied. Knowing this, television advertising around the world has come to be suffused with carefully crafted suggestions that happiness, social acceptance, success and respect are all necessarily associated with very high levels of material consumption.[29]

Over $500 billion is spend on global advertising every year.[30] The messages are increasingly flashing and beeping from our smartphones and tablets. The average American is exposed to over 350 different advertisements every day (but they only really notice about 150 of them).[31] Over a lifetime, the typical Briton spends more time watching TV than working.[32]

Advertising contains much more wealth, beauty and happiness than ordinary people will ever experience. As a result, the media is playing a bigger role than ever in shaping how we see our lives, the priorities we seek and choices we make. This cultural backdrop has a big impact on happiness.

We all know what the ads look like. The grinning dad who has a happier family because he bought that new car. The smiling mum whose kids rush to the table for a favourite meal. Even washing detergents seem to imply that cleaner clothes equals a happier family. Perfume, cars, fashion and food always appear to be bought by people who are more popular, better-looking, slimmer and above all happier than average.

The aspirational imagery is what sells products. The narrative that we would be happier if we bought more – and miserably deprived if we didn't – is what drives sales. The advertiser's job is typically to paint a picture of what life *could* be like. This technique of "comparative deprivation" is used to sell luxury goods as well as day-to-day products, increasingly in fast-growing and emerging markets.

When television first arrived in the tiny Kingdom of Bhutan, the changes that came about were alarming. A third of parents said they preferred watching TV to talking to their own children.[33] Robert Putnam's *Bowling Alone* famously blamed television for reducing civic activism and eroding social capital in America.[34]

When a significant technology diffuses widely, it often has an effect on wellbeing.[35] The arrival of the radio, television and now the internet changes the point of comparison. Instead of comparing to our village neighbours, we look to a global elite. When was the last time you saw an advert showing a 28-year-old Chinese man who earns less than $12,000 a year? That's the typical global citizen according to National Geographic.[36] But we never see that. Instead, most of the media portrays a life that's out of reach: richer, happier, healthier and more glamorous. The point is that this unfulfillable dream is changing the reference point for billions of people. For some, repeated exposure to the unfulfillable dream can't help but infuse a frustrating dissatisfaction. As a result, the media and consumer brands have come up for some heavy criticism.

An accusation of affluenza

Big brands are in the dock, accused of spreading misery through endless, mindless shopping. According to critics, companies have created an unhealthy addiction to stuff. They are perpetuating a treadmill of rising expectations that simply cannot be met. Oliver James has likened this to a disease, an "affluenza," that's sweeping our world.[37]

There is strong evidence to support this. Buying more stuff does not seem to increase wellbeing.[38] High consumption of most products, foods, housing, cars – even medical care – is not associated with higher levels of happiness.[39] That impulse buying, so often regretted, is particularly detrimental.[40]

Materialistic people are generally less happy. In one amazing study, people who were more focused on extrinsic goals (such as money, image and fame) were found to be not just more miserable, but physically less well. They reported more backache, headaches and muscle pain. Those who were less focused on such goals were both happier and healthier.[41] There may be some truth in the accusation that materialism is not just making us miserable – but sick.

Luxury goods are a particular concern. The benefit of many high-value or "positional" goods is that they are out of reach of most people.[42] The economist Robert Frank has gone as far as to argue that making and selling luxury goods (such as yachts or expensive watches) is a zero-sum game. The happiness of the lucky few is offset by the frustration for those who can't afford them.[43]

Far from making our world happier, these brands are being accused of painting unfulfillable dreams and perpetuating unhappiness. For some, the solution is to dematerialize – reduce clutter and clear our minds.[44] We'll return to the thorny question of consumption and growth in the final chapter. But this anti-consumption story is not quite as simple as it seems. In order to understand the impact of marketing on wellbeing, we must stop and ask: what are we actually buying?

What we shop for

The bestselling product groups of all time are as follows:[45]

1 Sony's PlayStation;
2 Pfizer's Lipitor (a statin medication);
3 Toyota's Corolla car;
4 the *Star Wars* movie trilogy;
5 Apple's iPad;
6 Nintendo's *Mario Bros.* games;
7 Michael Jackson's *Thriller* album;
8 The *Harry Potter* books;
9 Apple's iPhone; and
10 the Rubik's cube.

What do you notice about this list? Almost every one of these products is bought to do something else: to enjoy an *experience*. They are almost all games, movies, gadgets, books or music. Buying what's called an experiential good is not like an ice cream – here one second, gone and forgotten the next. The story, film, song or device provides repeated enjoyment over periods of time. They are often experiences that we share with others.

Far from wasting money on feckless fashions or unfulfilling treats, most purchases in the world are investments in entertaining experiences. After the essentials (such as housing, energy and food), most disposable income is spent on travel, eating out and entertainment.[46]

Purchases made "to do" are much better for wellbeing than those made "to have."[47] Buying experiences – or products that create an experience – brings higher levels of satisfaction because we immerse ourselves. Think about when you read a book, listen to music, enjoy a meal with friends or travel somewhere amazing. You are focused on enjoying the experience, the "flow,"[48] and also creating memories. Recollecting experiences creates particular value.

Perhaps consumers aren't quite as stupid as the critics think. The hundreds of millions of people who have bought the Rubik's cube or seen the *Star Wars* movies have clearly experienced a lot of enjoyment. Pfizer's Lipitor medication has saved millions of lives – directly contributing to increased life satisfaction. Even Apple's technology and Toyota's cars have no doubt brought joy to many who are better connected as a result.[49]

When we look at the habits of our planet and see what people are spending their cash on, the criticism of consumption simply doesn't stack up. Mindless, hedonistic binging doesn't seem as widespread as some would have us believe. Buying some stuff really can contribute to happiness; some shopping *can* make us feel better. How else can we explain why brands sell the same goods to the same people day after day? If that fizzy drink or tube of toothpaste didn't bring unequivocal satisfaction, we would switch to a competitor or stop buying.

Moderate levels of consumption have been shown to raise wellbeing in some studies.[50] This is especially true for those who are more materialistic: buying expensive items seems to bring joy to those who value status the most.[51] Most people are intelligent and rational enough to know that they will get some satisfaction – now and in the future – from owning a PlayStation or a *Harry Potter* book or a Michael Jackson album. Although these purchases won't improve life satisfaction on their own, they might bring a smile, make a day less frustrating and create something positive to look back on. Shared with other people, experiences can also make our relationships more enjoyable, which in turn helps improve wellbeing further. We'll see exactly how to design experiences to boost wellbeing in the final chapter.

Desire drives happiness

It's not even the actual product experience that determines many purchases. It's the *expectation* of delight. Academics have shown that desire – wanting a product – is what motivates us to buy. We want to sink our teeth into the cake far more than we enjoy the experience of doing so. This is why so much marketing appeals to desirability, not the actual experience.

Now here's the fascinating twist: desire and motivation are actually great for wellbeing. Without motivation, life would be incredibly dull. A desire to better ourselves is what gets people out of bed in the morning. Motivation makes us want to live our lives to the full. Without this yearning to consume, our world would be a lot less happy. People wouldn't want to buy much, so wouldn't need to work, but also wouldn't care much for leisure, music, art, food, travel, spending time with loved ones and everything else that makes life worth living. All this means that, according to Dr Neil Thin, one of the few academics to have interrogated the link between marketing and happiness, "the promise of shopping" and the need to work for it "is a crucial driver of modern motivation, and hence a major cause of happiness."[52] The very *need* to shop seems to be making us all happier.

Although we are motivated by consumption, that doesn't mean that all shopping is good for wellbeing. There are different types of buying. Marketing for wellbeing requires us to think about what is being marketed, to whom, in what quantities and how regularly. Crucially, there are two very distinct types of happiness that marketing affects. When Coca-Cola promises us we will "open happiness," this doesn't mean the same thing as making us more satisfied with life. Most marketers, if they think about wellbeing at all, are muddling different ideas. To get to the bottom of this crucial distinction, we need to take a short trip back to ancient Greece.

Lessons from Greek philosophy

In the fourth century BCE, a landmark centre for learning was founded in Greece. Its aim was to promote a particularly seductive philosophy: life is for pleasure. Cyrenaics taught that we exist to enjoy. This means living one's life to avoid pain, and actively seeking pleasurable sensations. This later became known as hedonism.

Around the same time, a traveller in the eastern Aegean was developing his own thoughts on what made for a rounded life. Aristotle taught a very different view, namely that something called *eudaimonia* was the highest form of human good. *Eudaimonia* is often translated as "human flourishing." Like Plato, Aristotle believed that happiness wasn't something that fell from the gods. In order to be truly satisfied, we need good character, and to take action, exercising virtue and ambition. So, eudaimonic wellbeing involves more than just pleasure; it requires morals and seizing opportunities for personal growth and life enrichment.

What does this mean for marketing some 2,500 years later? Well, these two schools of ancient Greek thought are at the kernel of the modern muddle over wellbeing. As individuals, we instinctively know that there is a difference between passing enjoyment ("pleasure") and enduring life satisfaction ("wellbeing"). "Being happy" for the next hour is not the same thing as "living well" over the next decade. While the two may be linked, both are quite separately measurable. You can be excitedly joyous at any given moment and still live in misery, or be very content week by week but still have moments of real anger, frustration and sorrow.

When marketers talk about a brand stimulating happiness, almost all of them mean it in the hedonistic sense of instant gratification. Coca-Cola, the world's most consumed brand,[53] no doubt brings moments of happiness in this sense.

But it is quite a different thing to enhance long-term life satisfaction through producing and selling drinks.

True happiness requires a brand to deliver more than a moment of joy. The pleasure (hedonism) must not be at the expense of the vital ingredients of wellbeing. A Wellthy Company addresses the positive *and negative* impacts of the brand. We'll see in the final chapter how to undertake a wellbeing footprint to inform such a strategy.

Building brands for wellbeing

Building brands for wellbeing involves delivering instant gratification as well as long-term life satisfaction. It requires advertising differently and seeking new ways to enable consumers to reach life-fulfilling goals. A Wellthy Company uses the power of marketing to increase the wellbeing of consumers in several crucial ways.

First, a Wellthy Company tackles any short-term causes of pain. The experience of interacting with some companies can be one of agitation, anger or even distress. Call centres are a particular problem for some brands. Airlines and phone companies frequently top the "most frustrating" lists. It is often the lack of humanity and flexibility that makes some customer service experiences so appalling.[54]

Customer satisfaction begins with great service. The powerful link between customer experience and profitability is illustrated by Sears, the department store. In the 1990s, executives calculated an insightful chain of statistics. They worked out that more positive attitudes among staff *directly* led to higher customer satisfaction. Happier shoppers, in turn, led to higher sales. The calculations were so precise that they could even forecast how changes in employee attitudes would affect revenues.[55] At the point of purchase or interaction, customer happiness can provide a framework for thinking beyond standard measures such as Net Promoter Score (NPS).

A Wellthy Company calculates both short- and long-term customer happiness. This is not just customer satisfaction. We are seeking genuine delight from interacting with the business and its staff. The experience should create feelings of warmth and leave a positive emotional imprint on the shopper. Where possible, the brand should seek to leave a lasting legacy and play a part in delivering products and services that raise life satisfaction. We'll return to this theme of innovation for wellbeing in the final chapter.

Next, a Wellthy Company uses marketing differently. Unilever's Dove brand launched an innovative strategy in 2004: the Campaign for Real Beauty. It centred on the insight that women's bodies were naturally different. Dove wanted to challenge narrow definitions and stereotypes. They landed on the idea of "real beauty" and celebrated human variety. In doing so, Unilever seized a powerful agenda that has become a social mission for the brand: enhancing self-esteem.

Further campaigns highlighted the "onslaught" of media images that shape young girls' perceptions of beauty. A "pro-age" initiative champions the very opposite of youth. Research shows that perceptions of women have, slowly, started to change. Meanwhile, Dove's sales have grown from $2.5 billion when the campaign was launched to over $4 billion 10 years later.[56]

When it comes to marketing, the Wellbeing Purpose is all about helping people feel good about themselves and growing revenues in the process. Dove's mission for self-esteem is an example of how brands can delight shoppers with a great product and shift social perceptions that make life better at the same time.

Marketing differently also involves applying innovative technologies for social good. Social media can perpetuate insecurities. But it also has the power to strengthen happiness. Brands can use these mediums to promote messages of self-confidence and share insights into what makes for more fulsome relationships and a more fulfilled life.

Companies often rely on creating ever-higher levels of aspiration – stimulating consumers to "trade up" to the next product. But perpetuating the need for more can make some feel less satisfied with the present. It's all relative. If you've just bought the iPhone 7 and notice adverts for the next model up, you might view your shiny new gadget with a twinge of dissatisfaction. In small measures, no one loses sleep over mild dissatisfaction. What we should worry about is how millions of messages over a lifetime ram home the idea that we need to spend more money on more stuff to be happy.

Wellthy brands inject a healthy dose of honesty into their marketing. They seek to close the often wide gap between advertised promises and average experiences. The brand aspires for *every* experience to exceed expectations. Messages are tailored to avoid over-claiming. Buying a new car or perfume won't make relationships with loved ones any better – but it might serve both a practical function as well as an emotional one.

For example, Patagonia's campaign entitled "Don't buy this jacket" is one of the most famous examples of discouraging unnecessary consumption. Originally promoted for environmental reasons, it resulted in strong brand recognition. When it comes to promises of a better life, a Wellthy Company avoids misleading hype. Conversely, if there is something that really can be done to improve life, the business leads the way.

Nudging towards happiness

When was the last time you saw an advert for a sugary, caloried can of Pepsi? If you're in the UK, it's probably been well over a decade. That's because, back in 2005, the company took the bold decision to lead their marketing with Pepsi Max, the no-sugar variety. In a declining cola market, it was a tenacious move to define a low-calorie alternative that was attractive to both men and women.

Five years later, Pepsi launched a large 600 ml Pepsi Max bottle that retailed at the same price as their smaller full-sugar variety. The chief executive described this as "another nudge in the right direction for our consumers." But how much margin did Pepsi lose selling bigger bottles for the same price as smaller ones? None. In fact, it generated millions of pounds of extra revenues for the brand, which now accounts for more than 50% of Pepsi's sales.[57]

What Pepsi is doing is making it easier for people to buy the healthier option. By enabling consumers to realize the right choices for their wellbeing, a Wellthy Company plays its part in improving quality of life and creates new relationships in the process.

Brands guide our behaviours through the choices and messages they provide. In their bestselling book *Nudge*, Cass Sunstein and Richard Thaler describe how dramatically different outcomes can be induced simply by changing the frame of reference (or "choice architecture").[58]

Their ideas have gained rapid popularity among politicians. But marketers have been nudging consumers for decades. Marketing for social outcomes has been going on since the 1950s when family planning campaigns were launched in many developing countries. Ever since, marketers have recognized a role in changing behaviours to help achieve a bigger aim.

But what should we be nudging people towards? This is the big question when it comes to wellbeing. To answer it, we need remind ourselves what the science shows does most to boost life satisfaction. In Chapter 2, we looked at what makes the average person happier in the long run: good mental and physical health, strong social relationships, safety and security, personal autonomy, and a sense of self-worth.

Wellthy brands boost wellbeing by nudging consumers to realize these aspirations. For example, a Wellthy Company might play a role in helping people to stay in touch with friends and family, exercise more, eat and drink more healthily, take medicines regularly, feel more empowered and confident, or volunteer in the community. Once we understand that wellbeing is measurable and changeable, there's no limit to what brands might do to make our world a little bit happier.

Of course, no brand can really claim to make life more satisfied for any one individual. But that's not the point. Some companies are currently eroding wellbeing. Some are trying to play their part in improving it. The new wellbeing economy is going to ask questions of companies in the former camp and reward ones in the latter. New relationships with customers can be built by making life feel better. The potential for companies to exert a powerful influence as an enabler and motivator for life goals is too big an opportunity to ignore.

Real preferences

When Nintendo launched the Wii in 2006, it faced intense competition from Microsoft's Xbox and Sony's PlayStation. Rather than playing up the classic image of sedentary teenagers, Nintendo landed on a dramatically different niche for gaming: family time. "We produce the action, YOU produce the fun" became the slogan. It was illustrated with pictures of families enjoying time together on the Wii. This was an abrupt departure from traditional games marketing, with a new target market of families.

Sales of the Wii in a single month broke all records in the US.[59] It was followed by the launch of the Wii Fit with balance board, which homed in on the idea that fitness is enjoyable and for everyone. This was sharply at odds with the classic image of a games console – a daring attempt to redefine a whole category. Wii Fit has become one of the bestselling products ever. Nintendo took a problem (lazy kids opting out of family time and exercise) and flipped it round through the brand (gaming is about quality family time and staying fit).[60]

Ask any marketing executive and they'll tell you that our stated preferences (what we say we want) often differ from our revealed preferences (what we actually do). We also have what are called meta-preferences, a kind of higher-order, longer-term set of aspirations: what we *really* want for our future.[61] Sometimes our preferences and meta-preferences appear contradictory. We may aspire to keep fit but pass a week without exercise, or believe in spending more time with family but fail to leave the office before 9 p.m. for months on end.

Sometimes the tension is between something pleasurable, such as eating very expensive chocolate, and another goal – saving money or getting healthier through avoiding treats. This type of tension is perfectly normal. Some people even exhibit a curious counter-phenomenon. They strive for a big goal at the expense of pleasure, such as someone training for a marathon when suffering from flu. Painful but purposeful. We have all sorts of preferences at different levels, often pointing in different directions.

There is an enormous opportunity for brands to unlock our meta-preferences. For any one person, the big life goals may need discovering. If you've never cooked from scratch or exercised regularly, how do you know if you'd like it? The marketing industry is skilled at identifying unmet and unarticulated needs. Marketers are particularly well placed to help spot and enable aspirations that are great for wellbeing.

When there is a tension between our short and long-term preferences, brands need to help find a realistic balance.[62] For companies selling potentially addictive things (such as some foods, drinks, cigarettes, gambling – even credit cards), it comes down to behaviour change. Honest advertising and product labelling are essential to persuading users that these products are best enjoyed responsibly and in moderation.

For foods, portion control is now an established means to encourage consumers to do what's best for their long-term wellbeing. Confectioners such as Mondelez (who make Cadbury's chocolate) and Ferrero have both pledged to reduce portion sizes to help people snack at the pace they want to.[63]

When asked about the future – what we want to do next week, for example – we are typically more generous to others, healthier in our choices and generally less lazy than when we are asked what we want right now. That's the meta-preferences surfacing. For most people, what they *say* they want in the weeks, months and years ahead aligns pretty closely with what's best for long-term well-being. Conversely, it's what we actually *do* that betrays our hedonic side and undermines our good intentions.[64] Thought of this way, it is not paternalistic or sinister for brands to help us realize our innermost desires.[65] It's simply effective marketing that will make us happier.

The debate over whether marketing makes life feel better or worse will rumble on. For foods marketed to children, such as the Happy Meal, the argument is particularly acute. That takes us back to Monet Parham, who is not all that she seems to be. As an employee of the California Department of Public Health, where she worked on nutrition, her lawsuit was backed by the Center for Science in the Public Interest. A judge ultimately threw out the case. Even Sarah Palin, the former Governor of Alaska, weighed into the debate on kids' nutrition, asking where responsibility really lay: "Should it be the government or should it be the parents? It should be the parents!" she cried to cheering supporters.

McDonald's were clearly miffed with all the attention, arguing that the lawsuit "only detracts from meaningful conversations about children's wellbeing."[66] To be fair, McDonald's have made great strides to improve the nutritional profile of their children's meals. They now offer healthier alternatives as part of the Happy Meal. That's the right response because for all the advertising, nudging, labelling and messaging, fundamentally this isn't really about selling. We must take a long hard look at *what* is being sold. The idea of designing products for wellbeing is something that we return to in the final chapter.

Few businesses seriously consider their impacts on customer happiness beyond the promises of a jolly strapline. But the potential for brands to make our world happier is immense. It's time for a rethink. A Wellthy Company brings joy in the instant and plays a part in enhancing life more substantively. That promise can drive a passionate affinity with a brand. Loyalty can generate repeat purchases, ensuring that the products and experiences that raise wellbeing further are consumed more and more.

A Wellthy Company reviews its advertising to see whether it's perpetuating feelings of frustration, anxiety and dissatisfaction – including among those who cannot afford the products. Campaigns are redefined to promote a more realistic image, and trigger actions that lead to more satisfaction, better self-esteem, improved health and stronger relationships. Advertising is designed to make people feel good and get more out of life. Finally, marketers should use their skills to test whether all this actually makes a difference.[67] Does viewing the advertising and buying and using the product really make any difference to life? For a single purchase, the contribution may be tiny. For the world's biggest brands, the sum total could be huge.

The science must guide the story. Brands need to be honest about what they are selling. They must be truthful about the benefits and whether a product really will bring the promised results. Sometimes that means marketing must recognize the limits and any downsides to what's being sold. But the need for truth is not limited to the marketing department. It extends to further responsibilities in our Wellbeing Purpose: behaving ethically, building trust and investing for happiness in communities.

Notes

1 Bayers, C. (1999). The inner Bezos. *Wired*, 3 January. Retrieved 24 March 2018, from www.wired.com/1999/03/bezos-3/.
2 Nies, Y. D. & Behrendt, T. (2010). Mom to sue McDonald's in Happy Meal battle. *ABC News*, 15 December. Retrieved 2 October 2016, from http://abcnews.go.com/US/mom-sue-mcdonalds-happy-meal-battle/story?id=12400445.
3 Technomic (2009). *Kids and Moms Consumer Trend Report*. Retrieved 2 October 2016, from www.technomic.com/_files/products/2009_kidsmoms_brochure_low_res.pdf.
4 McDonald's (2016). *Annual Report 2016*. Chicago, IL: McDonald's.
5 Ibid.
6 Schlosser, E. (2002). *Fast Food Nation: What the All-American Meal is Doing to the World*. London: Penguin.
7 Physicians Committee for Responsible Medicine (2018). *Childhood Lost: How the Happy Meal Can Lead to Diabetes, Obesity, and Hypertension*. Retrieved 24 February 2018, from www.pcrm.org/health/reports/happy-meal-leads-to-obesity.
8 Although seemingly replaced with "Taste the Feeling" in 2016, the "Open Happiness" message lives on in some markets.
9 Mazumdar, S. (2008). China and the global Atlantic: sugar from the age of Columbus to Pepsi-Coke and ethanol. *Food and Foodways*, 16(2), 135–147; www.cityweekend.com.cn/beijing/Word_SoftDrinks, accessed 16 October 2015.
10 Thin, N. (2012). *Social Happiness: Theory into Policy and Practice*. Bristol: Policy Press.
11 Chang, H. H. & Nayga Jr, R. M. (2010). Childhood obesity and unhappiness: the influence of soft drinks and fast food consumption. *Journal of Happiness Studies*, 11(3), 261–275.
12 Hoebel, B. G. (1982). The neural and chemical basis of reward: new discoveries and theories in brain control of feeding, mating, aggression, self-stimulation and self-injection. *Journal of Social and Biological Structures*, 5(4), 397–408.
13 Johnson, P. M. & Kenny, P. J. (2010). Addiction-like reward dysfunction and compulsive eating in obese rats: role for dopamine D2 receptors. *Nature Neuroscience*, 13(5), 635–641.
14 Chang, H. H. & Nayga Jr, R. M. (2010). Childhood obesity and unhappiness: the influence of soft drinks and fast food consumption. *Journal of Happiness Studies*, 11(3), 261–275.

15 Gilbert, D. T., Gill, M. J. & Wilson, T. D. (2002). The future is now: temporal correction in affective forecasting. *Organizational Behavior and Human Decision Processes*, *88*(1), 430–444.

16 Kahneman, D. & Thaler, R. H. (2006). Anomalies: utility maximization and experienced utility. *Journal of Economic Perspectives*, *20*(1), 221–234.

17 Institute for Fiscal Studies (2015). *How Do Payday Loans Affect UK Consumers?* Retrieved 26 February 2018, from www.ifs.org.uk/events/1229.

18 With Amos Tversky; for example, see Tversky, A. & Kahneman, D. (1974). Judgment under uncertainty: heuristics and biases. *Science*, *185*(4157), 1124–1131.

19 Perring, R. (2015). Britain's fattest: 65st man the size of four baby elephants is eating his way to death. *Daily Express*, 1 May.

20 DellaVigna, S. & Malmendier, U. (2002). *Overestimating Self-Control: Evidence from the Health Club Industry*. Stanford GSB Research Paper No. 1880. Retrieved 13 June 2018, from http://ssrn.com/abstract=347520.

21 Stutzer, A. & Frey, B. S. (2006). *What Happiness Research Can Tell Us about Self-Control Problems and Utility Misprediction*. Institute for Empirical Research in Economics Working Paper (267).

22 Loewenstein, G., Read, D. & Baumeister, R. F. (eds.) (2003). *Time and Decision: Economic and Psychological Perspectives of Intertemporal Choice*. New York: Russell Sage Foundation.

23 Wilson, T. D. & Gilbert, D. T. (2005). Affective forecasting: knowing what to want. *Current Directions in Psychological Science*, *14*(3), 131–134.

24 Merzer, M. (2016). *Survey: 3 in 4 Americans Make Impulse Purchases*. Retrieved 7 January 2017, from www.creditcards.com/credit-card-news/impulse-purchase-survey.php.

25 Redfin (2015). *1 in 4 American Homeowners Have Buyer's Remorse about Current Home, According to Nationwide Survey*. Retrieved 7 January 2017, from www.redfin.com/blog/2014/04/1-in-4-homeowners-have-buyers-remorse.html#.VhN6JlV4XCQ.

26 Galbraith, J. K. (1958). *The Affluent Society*. London: Hamish Hamilton.

27 Thin, N. (2012). *Social Happiness: Theory into Policy and Practice*. Bristol: Policy Press.

28 Bayers, C. (1999). The inner Bezos. *Wired*, 3 January. Retrieved 24 March 2018, from www.wired.com/1999/03/bezos-3/.

29 McDonald, R. (2004). Television, materialism and culture: an exploration of imported media and its implications for GNH. *Journal of Bhutan Studies*, *11*(1), 68–89.

30 Statista (2017). *GroupM Project That Global Advertising Spending Was $547.37 Billion in 2017*. Retrieved 16 November 2017, from www.statista.com/statistics/236943/global-advertising-spending/.

31 Media Dynamics Inc. (2014). *Adults Spend Almost 10 Hours per Day with the Media, but Note Only 150 Ads*. Retrieved 28 February 2018, from www.mediadynamicsinc.com/uploads/files/PR092214-Note-only-150-Ads-2mk.pdf.

32 Layard, R. (2011). *Happiness: Lessons from a New Science*. London: Penguin. Lord Layard cites the *Journal of Bhutan Studies* for this story.

33 Ibid.

34 Putnam, R. D. (2001). *Bowling Alone: The Collapse and Revival of American Community*. New York: Simon & Schuster.

35 Layard, R. (2011). *Happiness: Lessons from a New Science*. London: Penguin.

36 National Geographic (2011). *Seven Billion: Are You Typical?* Retrieved 27 February 2018, from http://video.nationalgeographic.com/video/news/7-billion/ngm-7billion-typical.

37 James, O. (2007). *Affluenza: How to Be Successful and Stay Sane*. London: Random House.

38 Ng, Y. K. (2002). Economic policies in the light of happiness studies with reference to Singapore. *The Singapore Economic Review*, 47(2), 199–212.

39 DeLeire, T. & Kalil, A. (2010). Does consumption buy happiness? Evidence from the United States. *International Review of Economics*, 57(2), 163–176.

40 Silvera, D. H., Lavack, A. M. & Kropp, F. (2008). Impulse buying: the role of affect, social influence, and subjective wellbeing. *Journal of Consumer Marketing*, 25(1), 23–33.

41 Kasser, T. (2003). *The High Price of Materialism*. Cambridge, MA: MIT Press.

42 Hirsch, F. (1976). *Social Limits to Growth*. Cambridge, MA: Harvard University Press.

43 Frank, R. H. (1999). *Luxury Fever: Money and Happiness in an Era of Excess*. Princeton, NJ: Princeton University Press.

44 Wallman, J. (2015). *Stuffocation: Why We've Had Enough of Stuff and Need Experience More Than Ever*. New York: Spiegel & Grau.

45 Calculated from unit sales total by category. Calio, V., Frohlich, T. & Hess, A. E. M. (2014). These are the 10 best-selling products of all time. *Time*, 8 May.

46 For example, Office of National Statistics (2014). *Family Spending Release*. London: Office of National Statistics.

47 Van Boven, L. & Gilovich, T. (2003). To do or to have? That is the question. *Journal of Personality and Social Psychology*, 85(6), 1193–1202; Guevarra, D. A. & Howell, R. T. (2015). To have in order to do: exploring the effects of consuming experiential products on well-being. *Journal of Consumer Psychology*, 25(1), 28–41.

48 Csikszentmihalyi, M. (1996). *Flow and the Psychology of Discovery and Invention*. New York: HarperCollins.

49 Bettingen, J. F., & Luedicke, M. K. (2009). Can brands make us happy? A research framework for the study of brands and their effects on happiness. *Advances in Consumer Research*, 36(1), 308–315.

50 Veenhoven, R. (2004). *Sustainable Consumption and Happiness*. Rotterdam: Erasmus University.

51 Hudders, L. & Pandelaere, M. (2012). The silver lining of materialism: the impact of luxury consumption on subjective well-being. *Journal of Happiness Studies*, 13(3), 411–437.

52 Thin, N. (2012). *Social Happiness: Theory into Policy and Practice*. Bristol: Policy Press.

53 Kantar Worldpanel (2013). *A Global Ranking of the Most Chosen Consumer Brands*. London: Kantar.

54 Hilton, S., Bade, S. & Bade, J. (2016). *More Human: Designing a World Where People Come First*. New York: PublicAffairs.

55 Rucci, A. J., Kirn, S. P. & Quinn, R. T. (1998). The employee-customer-profit chain at Sears. *Harvard Business Review*, 76, 82–98.

56 Neff., J. (2014). Ten years in, Dove's "Real Beauty" seems to be aging well. *Advertising Age*. Retrieved 13 June 2018, from http://adage.com/article/news/ten-years-dove-s-real-beauty-aging/291216/.

57 North, A. (2015). Health matters: Brits splash out on low and no cal drinks. *The Grocer*, 27 March; Thomas, J. (2010). Pepsi gives sugar free consumers more for their money. *Campaign*, February.

58 Thaler, R. H. & Sunstein, C. R. (1998). *Nudge: Improving Decisions about Health, Wealth, and Happiness*. New Haven, CT: Yale University Press.

59 Kohler, C. (2010). December NPD: the Nintendo that stole Christmas. *Wired*, 14 October.

60   Various sources, including Guild, T., Kepski, M. & Simonides, M. (2012). *Nintendo Wii Marketing Plan*. Retrieved 5 February 2017, from www.slideshare.net/mjk3491/nintendo-wii-marketing-plan.

61   Frankfurt, H. G. (1971). Freedom of the will and the concept of a person. *Journal of Philosophy, 68*, 5–20.

62   Desmet, P. M. & Pohlmeyer, A. E. (2013). Positive design: an introduction to design for subjective well-being. *International Journal of Design, 7*(3), 5–19.

63   Nieburg, O. (2014). Reducing portion sizes: cutting calories or cheating consumers? *Confectionary News*, 25 November; Harrison-Dunn, A. (2013). Don't change our treats! Smaller portions better than reformulation for confectionery, says dietitian. *Confectionary News*, 28 October.

64   Fischer, E. F. (2014). *The Good Life: Aspiration, Dignity, and the Anthropology of Wellbeing*. Stanford, CA: Stanford University Press.

65   Locke, J. (1836). *An Essay Concerning Human Understanding*. London: T. Tegg & Son.

66   Reuters Staff (2011). McDonald's loses bid to move Happy Meal lawsuit-judge. *Reuters*, 20 July. Retrieved 4 March 2016, from www.reuters.com/article/mcdonalds-lawsuit-idUSN1E76J0XM20110720.

67   For ideas on how to measure brand happiness, see Bettingen, J. F. & Luedicke, M. K. (2009). Can brands make us happy? A research framework for the study of brands and their effects on happiness. *Advances in Consumer Research, 36*(1), 308–315.

Chapter 7

Trust

Ethics and the community

If you want happiness for an hour, take a nap.

If you want happiness for a day, go fishing.

If you want happiness for a year, inherit a fortune.

If you want happiness for a lifetime, help someone else.

Chinese proverb[1]

It was a damp morning in Luxembourg when the phone call came. Alistair Darling, the UK's Chancellor of the Exchequer, was rushed out of a European Finance Ministers' meeting. Aides hastily cleared a side room to take this call. On the line was Tom McKillop, chairman of the world's largest bank at the time, the Royal Bank of Scotland (RBS). Darling later described this moment in October 2008 when a chill went down his spine. McKillop revealed that the bank was haemorrhaging cash. His firm couldn't last long. The government was already preparing a bailout package. But it would take time.

Darling then asked the killer question: "How long have you got?" "Maybe two or three hours," came the reply. Darling quickly realized the massive implications. If confidence failed in the world's largest bank, chaos could follow. He made a mad dash back to London by plane, making phone calls to the governor of the Bank of England and other financial leaders to shore up support for the economy.

In his memoirs, Darling recalled this historic phone call as the moment that the possibility crossed his mind of "complete economic and therefore social collapse . . . It was rather like nuclear war . . . you think it will never happen. And then someone tells you that a missile's been launched."[2]

The global financial crisis rocked our faith in banks and big business. It was only due to a historic part nationalization of RBS – a £37 billion bailout – that catastrophe was averted. American taxpayers faced their own horrors when the government had to prop up AIG to the tune of $170 billion.

Over a decade later, the blame game goes on. Regulators had clearly taken their eyes off the ball. Governments should bear much of the responsibility. But it was actions by individuals working in companies that ultimately undermined a vital commodity: trust. RBS succeeded in becoming, in the words of one of its leaders, the "least trusted company in the least trusted sector."[3] The financial crisis illustrates perfectly how without trust, the economy simply cannot function.

Back in the 1980s, nearly 90% of British people said that they thought banks were "well run." Following the RBS collapse and Lehman Brothers bankruptcy, the numbers saying that they trusted banks fell to just 21% in the UK and US.[4] Harris Interactive found that just 6% of Americans felt that Wall Street firms were honest and trustworthy.[5]

This free fall in confidence was one of the most dramatic transformations in public attitudes ever seen.[6] The automotive sector was next, when the US government rescued General Motors and Chrysler. Then scandals such as Bernie Madoff's $65 billion Ponzi fraud spread disillusionment. The number of people saying that they trusted business dipped to its lowest levels in decades.[7]

But what's all this got to do with happiness? The really interesting thing is that the pollsters found it wasn't just trust in business that fell. In the darkest months that followed the collapse of many household names, citizens lost faith in one and other. We began to trust our neighbours less. There was a rise in the number of people agreeing that "most people try to take advantage of me."[8] Bad behaviours by business – and the regulators and ratings agencies that appeared asleep on the job – eroded trust in communities at large.

The value of trust

Every time we buy food from a store or order anything online, we are putting our trust in business. We trust companies to sell us meals that are safe to eat and fulfil their promises to deliver us goods. Without trust, commerce would seize up. A high-trust environment is crucial for economic progress. When we trust others, we can cooperate, build relationships over time and avoid costly controls.

Trust is essential for wellbeing to flourish. The happiest communities aren't the richest ones. The happiest people live in societies where confidence in others is high, institutions are effective and corruption is low.[9] Those who say that they trust others, participate in the community, perceive society to be fair and generally feel safe are always much happier – no matter what the culture or country.[10]

Feeling like we belong to a community, and can rely on others, creates a positive glow that's hard to replicate. When we experience high levels of confidence in each other, neuroscientists have found that our brains release a hormone – oxytocin – that literally makes cooperation feel good.[11]

Regularly having conversations with neighbours significantly increases life satisfaction.[12] Conversely, when we say loneliness is painful, it's more than just a metaphor. Experiencing social isolation affects the same parts of the brain as physical discomfort.[13]

The role for business in trust-building is pivotal. For example, research has shown that being able to trust banks and business people has a positive relationship with feeling good about life.[14] The global financial crisis illustrated how when the actions are big and bad enough, there are knock-on effects across communities. As we lost trust in one and other, businesses stopped investing. They stopped hiring. The job statistics tell one story. But the wellbeing data reveal an even more powerful tale.

Around the world, hundreds of millions more people rated the quality of their life just 4 or lower out of 10.[15] As the recession began to bite, scores reached a nadir in the US in 2010 when the American General Social Survey recorded its lowest ever results for happiness.[16] It's no coincidence that wellbeing and trust scores fell at the same time. A feeling that businesses were in it for themselves, and couldn't be trusted to act responsibly, was one contributor to a climate of declining quality of life.

There's an expression used to describe this glue that binds us together: social capital. Social capital is an invisible web of bonds that links people and institutions. Through their everyday actions, companies can extend and deepen this network, as well as erode and undermine it.

In the previous chapter, we saw how Wellthy brands deliver on their promises. How much we trust a brand is shaped by reputation, perceived quality and our own experience. When we engage with a brand – such as using a product or experiencing a service – levels of trust are affected by the quality of the interaction.

Did the brand perform as we expected? Did the company behind it live up to our expectations? If a business fails to deliver what's expected, people remember it. Conversely, when consumers trust a brand, they return to it time and again. According to surveys, four in five Americans would recommend a brand and purchase it regularly if they trusted it.[17]

A Wellthy Company builds faith in business through delivering what's promised alongside great customer service. Safe, accessible, valued and consistently great products isn't rocket science. Why does this matter for happiness? It's not just the wellbeing of the individual customer we are concerned with. Instead, it's the knock-on effects. When companies deliver fantastic solutions, they build confidence that helps society to function. But it's when a business utterly fails to live up to social standards that the real influence of business on wellbeing emerges.

The madness of men

The rumour on the street was that the share price had reached unsustainable levels. From their headquarters in Threadneedle Street, in the heart of the City of London, the directors pushed ahead with ever-more daring claims. Lies inspired further deceit as the share price doubled, tripled, quadrupled then soared again to well over 600% in gains.

The leadership of the firm deliberately whipped up hyperbole in the newspapers. The true finances of the business were hidden from the world in an elaborate deception. Accounting books were doctored. Insider dealing was rife. Senior politicians were secretly sold shares at a discounted price – then encouraged to vote through fantastical laws that expanded the business's monopoly. This was a speculative frenzy driven by fraud.

Shares in the South Sea Company finally collapsed in September 1720. Britain's greatest stock market bubble caused widespread panic, bankruptcy, poverty and contagion that spread across early eighteenth-century Europe.[18] The speculative financing of Britain's debt – to explore what were called the South Seas and is now South America – illustrates how shared norms are essential for business to function properly. You can't have an effective commercial relationship without faith that all parties can be relied upon to act ethically.

Parliament's subsequent report into the scandal revealed massive fraud and corruption among the company directors and several government ministers. The devastation ran deep in London society – even the king's mistresses lost money. Sir Isaac Newton was among the great names that were caught up, making his famous lament: "I can calculate the movement of the stars, but not the madness of men."[19]

Every time a company lies, has a safety breach or misleads a customer, it breeds the type of cynicism that erodes confidence, undermines communities and chips away at wellbeing. Misleading advertising, cheating the system, unethical lobbying, faulty products and outright discrimination all fuel the feeling that business – and people "round here" – just can't be trusted.

That's exactly what we saw with the global financial crisis: people didn't just lose trust in business, but also each other. When companies let society down, they erode the confidence that binds communities together. When companies don't pay their fair share of taxes, people start thinking that businesses are cheating the system at their expense. All this affects happiness because when trust is low, wellbeing cannot thrive.

Checks and balances are essential to prevent unethical behaviour running rampant. The madness of men (and it's normally men) can be curtailed by laws. But most commerce functions on voluntary standards and norms. A shared sense of what is right and wrong is essential for trust to blossom.

An ethical environment is essential to cultivate both wellbeing and wealth creation. Values such as honesty, openness and decency enable relationships both within the company, and outside of it, to grow through mutual respect. Without respect, there is no trust. Without trust, there can be no happiness.

The automotive industry has been in the firing line for spreading this cynicism. For companies such as Volkswagen, apparently endemic attempts to game the emissions tests and mislead authorities have done much damage to corporate reputation. From Enron's accounting fraud to BP's safety lapses at Deepwater Horizon, there are countless examples of big business causing major trust ripples. By eroding confidence in society, corporate scandals chip away and damage wellbeing at large.

Trust in business is a vital and pressing issue today. Less than half the populations of most countries – from Australia to the UK – say that they trust companies. America saw the biggest freefall in confidence (a massive 10 percentage points) from 2017 to 2018, according to the Edelman Trust Barometer.[20] It is essential for business to play a proactive role in rebuilding confidence in commerce.

Corruption

Corruption is a particularly potent destroyer of wellbeing. Bribery can be perpetrated by wayward businesses just as much as dodgy government officials. Corruption is the world's most talked about global problem, according to a BBC study.[21] Surveys suggest that four in five people on the planet believe graft to be a problem in their country.[22]

Corruption has an extraordinary impact on wellbeing. Multiple studies have found a significant link between how crooked a society is perceived to be and how happy its citizens report they are.[23] Companies can play a part in mitigating misery by putting in place mechanisms to stamp out corrupt practices and promote good governance.

A written code of ethics can help – covering issues such as conflicts of interest, gifts, hospitality and lobbying. But it must be implemented through training, enforced through sanctions and enabled through whistleblowing. Above all, moral behaviours must be underpinned by culture. Values such as tolerance, respect for others, civic participation, personal integrity and openness can all build social capital and reduce the risk of ethical violations.

Transparency around business practices can build confidence. But all too often, communication by companies takes the form of anecdotal success stories. Instead, a Wellthy Company tells the world what happens when things *don't* go to plan. This includes reporting on breaches of codes of conduct, or performance when a target has been missed.

Honesty deepens the trust reserves. Explaining the reasons why progress has been slow can create a culture of learning and mutual respect. In fact, it's when things really don't go to plan, when there is a true crisis that threatens the very existence of the firm, that we really see how serious a business is about trust and wellbeing.

Credo in a crisis

The chairman and president settled down for their regular catch-up on the fifth floor of their New Jersey headquarters on 30 September 1982. Johnson & Johnson (J&J) was one of the world's most successful drug makers. But a few floors down in the PR department, the phones began ringing. Journalists kept calling all morning. Some catastrophic news was filtering through from Chicago about a series of suspicious deaths.

"Are you sure this isn't a hoax?" demanded one executive when he was told the news. According to the callers, cyanide – a lethal poison – had been found in Tylenol, J&J's biggest painkiller. The death toll was rising. A 12-year-old girl was the latest victim and it quickly became clear that it was time to let the bosses know.

The senior leadership meeting on the fifth floor was dramatically adjourned. As police confirmed that several batches of Extra Strength Tylenol had been contaminated with poison, a nationwide panic erupted. With it, a full-blown corporate crisis unfolded. Shops rushed to remove the brand from their shelves. Concerned consumers overwhelmed poison control hotlines. The police in Chicago took the extraordinary step of driving through the streets blasting out warnings on loudhailers not to take Tylenol.[24]

Trust in the brand collapsed overnight. The J&J share price plunged by a fifth. Pundits questioned whether the company could survive. But J&J knew that the Tylenol deaths could not be the firm's fault. They quickly ascertained that batches from different factories had been contaminated. A murderer – who was never caught – was tampering with the product *after* it had reached the stores.

David Clare, the J&J president, later described an "ethical dilemma" that was playing out in his mind. Should the business withdraw its most profitable product from stores nationwide, and show that any madman could bring a brand to its knees? Or should they keep the tablets on the shelves, and risk further deaths?[25]

James Burke, the chairman, turned to a historic source for inspiration. In 1943, just before the company was listed on the stock exchange, the then CEO, Robert Wood Johnson, penned "Our Credo." This unique philosophy outlined the values of the business, beginning with a promise to put patients, doctors and all those who used their products first.[26] Burke later described how the credo gave him the testimony he needed to persuade shareholders to back a massive nationwide recall of 31 million containers – at a cost of $100 million.[27]

The amazing thing about J&J's decision was that there was no regulatory requirement to recall the product. There was also no doubt that the company wasn't responsible for the contamination. But the values that were codified in their credo made it clear that consumers had to come first. It seemed like the right course of action to restore faith in the brand.

J&J's response is now the textbook example of how to deal with a crisis in trust. Executives were put up for a campaign of media interviews. Burke led the charge with a forthrightness and honesty that was met with widespread praise.[28] Toll-free helplines were set up. Half a million mail shots were sent to health professionals. A $100,000 reward was offered to help catch the killer responsible. And 160 visits were made to congressional offices to lobby to make product-tampering harder. Taken together, over 125,000 news clippings were generated – more than any other incident since the assassination of John F. Kennedy. This media blitz did huge amounts to reduce worry, build confidence and cement trust not just in J&J, but other healthcare businesses too.[29]

Within 10 weeks, the brand was back on the shelves with new, triple-seal, tamper-resistant packaging. Discount pricing was accompanied by thousands of presentations to the medical community. Trust was restored. Pundits had predicted that the brand would never recover. But within a year, Tylenol's market share – which had collapsed from 37% to just 7% of the analgesic market – had staged an astonishing comeback to 30%.[30]

If you make painkillers, few things can be worse than a nationwide panic from poison contamination. It's a reminder of the first priority of a Wellthy Company: reliable and safe products that deliver what they promise. But J&J's response shows how values and the right actions can help weather a storm, rebuild faith and restore market share. Years later, Burke reflected on this: "You tell me any human relationship that works without trust, whether it is a marriage or a friendship or a social interaction; in the long run, the same thing is true about business."[31]

The biggest lesson from the Tylenol response is that when things don't go the plan, sensible honesty is vital to restoring confidence. Many companies have a pathological fear of openness. They worry that airing their dirty laundry – lifting the lid on the challenges and frustrations felt behind closed doors – makes them appear weak. In fact, the opposite is often true. Most people – particularly the informed stakeholders that lead public opinion – respect openness far more than they discredit things not going to plan. Secrecy that veils a scandal is often far worse than opening up to talk about problems early on.

How companies behave, and their response to a crisis, tells you a lot about their commitment to trust. A Wellthy Company engenders faith in the firm. But there is a big difference between defending one brand and enhancing social capital more widely. Business is part of a wider web of transactions that affect happiness. In order to really strengthen wellbeing, there is one final component to building community bonds: social investment in happiness.

Social investment in happiness

Given the choice between spending money on yourself or someone else, which would you rather do? Studies suggest that spending cash on other people is much better for our happiness. Splashing out on friends, for example, has been shown to generate more positive feelings than spending on yourself.[32]

Altruism is hardwired into our nature. In his book *Flourish*, Martin Seligman showed how a single daily act of kindness produces more happiness than any other activity.[33] That's why, Seligman advises, we should all regularly practise generosity to improve how we feel about life.

A Wellthy Company invests in altruism by contributing to communities. This might be through charitable donations (including matching employee contributions), staff volunteering, pro bono support or marketing that is tied to a cause. But this isn't just old-fashioned CSR. Social investment in wellbeing requires ruthless targeting to maximize life satisfaction.

There is a cascade of benefits from social investment in happiness. First, the employee gains. Giving up your time or money to a good cause can create a large and lasting boost to wellbeing. In 120 out of 136 countries surveyed in the Gallup World Poll, respondents who had donated to charity in the last month reported greater life satisfaction.[34] Those who give up their time to volunteer are typically much happier.[35]

An altruistic outlook, caring about others and acting generously really does seem to increase optimism about life. This may be because it engenders an awareness of good fortune and helps people to see themselves from another perspective.[36]

Second, the recipients of the investment benefit. But too much corporate giving is scatter-gun. A Wellthy Company targets its community investment where it does the most to increase life satisfaction. This requires understanding the happiness footprint of the community and targeting beneficiaries with the lowest levels of wellbeing. Just as we saw in Chapter 4 on the supply chain, marginal groups such as minorities and the unemployed, especially women in disadvantaged communities, often have the lowest wellbeing.

Many businesses donate large sums to support cultural and artistic initiatives. This no doubt creates joy for countless people who experience the exhibits. Art can truly be life-changing. But it's nowhere near as life-changing as having safe drinking water if you are at risk of death, or shelter to sleep in when fleeing conflict. Some causes make a bigger difference than others. P&G, for example, has a partnership with UNICEF through its Pampers brand. This has seen 300 million vaccines given since 2006, helping to eliminate neonatal tetanus in 15 African countries.[37]

Effective altruism is a growing movement that calls on individuals to give money where it makes the biggest difference.[38] For a Wellthy Company, a wellbeing lens provides a new motivation to rethink contributions. We should ask: where can happiness be boosted the most? Would we rather substantively raise life satisfaction for a refugee without shelter, food or medicine — or create a smile and wonderful memory for an art lover? The moral case is clearly for the former. Investment in mental and physical health, social and family support and back-to-work programmes can all have direct and measurable impacts on how people feel about life. When it comes to happiness, we should be honest that not all causes are equal.

As well as a moral case, there is a business case for investing cash and time where it makes the biggest difference. Effective community investment can boost reputation and staff morale, reduce employee turnover, and create a sense of purpose and meaning. Studies suggest that raising satisfaction for employees doesn't flow from random volunteering. It comes from supporting causes that really make an impact and change lives.[39] In businesses where the social benefit of the company is not always clear, pro bono support for a worthy cause can create real purpose and value.[40]

A direct link between the business and the community boosts happiness all round. Strategic investment and effective volunteering builds social capital: strengthening the capacity of non-profits, and increasing trust and cooperation between employees, companies and community organizations.[41] Investing in happiness increases wellbeing for employees, the individuals that benefit and also communities in the round.

What about customers? Cause-related marketing can be a clever way to build trust as well as an emotional connection. By donating a small proportion of profits to a good cause, brands are able to shout about the social benefits in their marketing. But a note of caution is warranted here. Much cause-marketing is superficial – seeking the sales with little consideration of the value of the cause.

In their book *Happy Money*, Elizabeth Dunn and Michael Norton show that when shoppers focus on themselves ("what do I want to buy?") rather others ("what's the best cause to support?"), it can actually *reduce* happiness compared to just giving cash to charity.[42] The basis for cause-marketing needs to be genuinely impactful. The authors recommend that businesses:

> think about fostering the conditions that promote the warm glow of giving, structuring cause-marketing initiatives so that customers feel they are making a choice to support a cause, that they are connected to the beneficiaries, and that they are making a real impact.[43]

Since the dawn of commerce, the earliest traders knew that if they sold a dangerous product or cheated the customer, their credibility and future business could suffer. Many businesses still think that responsible behaviours are all about reducing the risk of being "found out." Doing the right thing is about protecting a licence to operate: diminishing the risk that misdemeanours might occur and damage reputation.

With the Wellbeing Purpose, the rationale for ethical business is quite different. It's about the actual consequences – for employees, victims of corporate abuse, beneficiaries and society at large. The motivation for action is that unethical behaviours result in unhappy people. Indignity, lying and cheating are not just wrong in the moral sense. They don't make for bad business just because of reputational risks either. These issues matter because of their consequences: individual misery as well as a weaker society.

By the same token, investing in communities should not be about supporting causes closest to home just because the chairman rates them. Effective altruism means asking some hard questions about *why* we are giving and *what* impact we want to have. Lots of companies talk about impact. Too few understand that social investment should really be about making life feel better for more people. What other impact is really of social value?

An ethical culture and social investment for happiness cannot be afterthoughts. They need to be part of a coherent whole. To deliver our ambitions for the Wellbeing Purpose, actions are required that transcend the entire corporation, and run deep into the DNA of the business model. This requires a strategic mindset: a corporate blueprint for life enhancement.

Notes

1   Stone, J. R. (2006). *The Routledge Book of World Proverbs*. London: Routledge.
2   Watkins, S. (2013). Britain was two hours away from total social collapse. *Mail on Sunday*, 7 September.
3   BBC News (2014). RBS: Ross McEwan speech in full. *BBC News*, 27 February. Retrieved 25 April 2017, from www.bbc.co.uk/news/business-your-money-26365616.
4   Figures for the UK are from Edelman (2010). *Edelman Trust Barometer*. New York: Edelman; and for the US from Gallup (n.d.). *Confidence in Institutions*. Washington, DC: Gallup. Retrieved 23 May 2017, from www.gallup.com/poll/1597/confidence-institutions.aspx.
5   Harris Interactive (2009). *Only One Quarter of Americans Say Banks Are Honest and Trustworthy*. Press release, 30 June.
6   National Centre for Social Research (2013). *British Social Attitudes Survey*. London: National Centre for Social Research.
7   Edelman (2009). *Edelman Trust Barometer*. London: Edelman.
8   ESS (2009). *European Social Survey 2009*. London: University of London.
9   Helliwell, J. F. (2003). How's life? Combining individual and national variables to explain subjective well-being. *Economic Modelling*, 20(2), 331–360.
10 Bjørnskov, C. (2007). Determinants of generalized trust: a cross-country comparison. *Public Choice*, 130(1), 1–21, cited in Dolan, P., Peasgood, T. & White, M. (2008). Do we really know what makes us happy? A review of the economic literature on the factors associated with subjective well-being. *Journal of Economic Psychology*, 29(1), 94–122; see also Graham, C. (2012). *Happiness around the World: The Paradox of Happy Peasants and Miserable Millionaires*. Oxford: Oxford University Press.
11 Trevino, L. K. & Nelson, K. A. (2010). *Managing Business Ethics*. Hoboken, NJ: John Wiley & Sons.
12 National Centre for Social Research (2013). *British Social Attitudes Survey*. London: National Centre for Social Research.
13 Helliwell, J. F., Layard, R. and Sachs, J. (eds.) (2015). *World Happiness Report 2015*. New York: Sustainable Development Solutions Network.
14 Leung, A., Kier, C., Fung, T., Fung, L. & Sproule, R. (2013). Searching for happiness: the importance of social capital. In A. Delle Fave (ed.), *The Exploration of Happiness* (pp. 247–267). Dordrecht: Springer.
15 The number of people telling Gallup that their life rated only 4 or less out of 10 rose from 9% in 2007 to 13% in 2009. Gallup (2012). *Nearly One in Four Worldwide Thriving*.

Retrieved 13 May 2017, from www.gallup.com/poll/153818/Nearly-One-Four-Worldwide-Thriving.aspx.

16 Smith, T. W., Marsden, P., Hout, M. & Kim, J. (2010). *General Social Survey, 2010*. Chicago, IL: NORC at the University of Chicago.

17 YEC Women (2014). Three ways to build customer trust. *Forbes*, 22 April.

18 Evans, R. (2014). The South Sea Bubble caused the largest crash ever recorded for British equities from peak to trough. The biggest stock market crashes in history. *Daily Telegraph*, 9 September.

19 Various sources, including Harvard Business School (n.d.). *South Sea Bubble Short History*. Cambridge, MA: Harvard Business School. Retrieved 13 June 2018, from www.library.hbs.edu/hc/ssb/history.html.

20 The general population trust index in the US for business has fallen from 58 in 2017 to 48 in 2018. Edelman (2018). *Edelman Trust Barometer 2018*. New York: Edelman.

21 BBC World Service (2010). Corruption is the most talked about global problem. *BBC News*, 9 December. Retrieved 13 June 2018, from www.bbc.co.uk/pressoffice/pressreleases/stories/2010/12_december/09/corruption.shtml.

22 Helliwell, J. F., Layard, R. and Sachs, J. (eds.) (2015). *World Happiness Report 2015*. New York: Sustainable Development Solutions Network.

23 For example, see Helliwell, J. F., Huang H. & Wang, S. (2017). The social foundations of world happiness. *World Happiness Report 2017*, 2, 8–46.

24 Knowledge@Wharton (2009). Tylenol and the legacy of J&J's James Burke. *Time*, 5 October.

25 Groucutt, J., Leadley, P. & Forsyth, P. (2004). *Marketing: Essential Principles, New Realities*. London: Kogan Page.

26 Lazare, L. (2002). Crisis triggered brilliant PR response. *Chicago Sun Times*, 29 September.

27 Pandya, M. & Shell, R. (2006) *Lasting Leadership*. Philadelphia, PA: Wharton School Publishing; Knowledge@Wharton (2009). Tylenol and the legacy of J&J's James Burke. *Time*, 5 October.

28 Rehak, J. (2002). Tylenol made a hero of Johnson & Johnson: the recall that started them all. *New York Times*, 23 March. Retrieved 11 July 2017, from www.nytimes.com/2002/03/23/your-money/tylenol-made-a-hero-of-johnson-johnson-the-recall-that-started.html.

29 Groucutt, J., Leadley, P. & Forsyth, P. (2004). *Marketing: Essential Principles, New Realities*. London: Kogan Page.

30 Rehak, J. (2002). Tylenol made a hero of Johnson & Johnson: the recall that started them all. *New York Times*, 23 March. Retrieved 11 July 2017, from www.nytimes.com/2002/03/23/your-money/tylenol-made-a-hero-of-johnson-johnson-the-recall-that-started.html.

31 Knowledge@Wharton (2009). Tylenol and the legacy of J&J's James Burke. *Time*, 5 October.

32 Aknin, L. B., Dunn, E. W. & Norton, M. I. (2012). Happiness runs in a circular motion: evidence for a positive feedback loop between prosocial spending and happiness. *Journal of Happiness Studies*, 13(2), 347–355.

33 Seligman, M. E. (2012). *Flourish: A Visionary New Understanding of Happiness and Well-Being*. New York: Simon & Schuster.

34 Dunn, E. & Norton, M. (2014). *Happy Money: The Science of Happier Spending*. New York: Simon & Schuster.

35 Meier, S. & Stutzer, A. (2008). Is volunteering rewarding in itself? *Economica*, 75(297), 39–59.

36 Lyubomirsky, S., Sheldon, K. M. & Schkade, D. (2005). Pursuing happiness: the architecture of sustainable change. *Review of General Psychology*, 9(2), 111–131.

37 P&G (n.d.). *Pampers Vaccination Program*. Retrieved 13 June 2017, from www.pg.com/en_US/sustainability/social_responsibility/health_hygiene/pampers_unicef.shtml.

38 MacAskill, W. (2015). *Doing Good Better: Effective Altruism and a Radical New Way to Make a Difference*. London: Guardian Faber Publishing; Singer, P. (2015). *The Most Good You Can Do: How Effective Altruism Is Changing Ideas about Living Ethically*. New Haven, CT: Yale University Press.

39 Dunn, E. & Norton, M. (2014). *Happy Money: The Science of Happier Spending*. New York: Simon & Schuster.

40 New Economics Foundation (2014). *Wellbeing at Work: A Review of the Literature*. London: New Economics Foundation.

41 Muthuri, J., Moon, J. & Matten, D. (2006). *Employee Volunteering and the Creation of Social Capital*. Nottingham: ICCSR.

42 Citing Krishna, A. (2011). Can supporting a cause decrease donations and happiness? The cause marketing paradox. *Journal of Consumer Psychology*, 21(3), 338–345.

43 Dunn, E. & Norton, M. (2014). *Happy Money: The Science of Happier Spending*. New York: Simon & Schuster.

Chapter 8

Strategy
A business model for life

> Action may not always bring happiness; but there is no happiness without action.
>
> Benjamin Disraeli, British Prime Minister (1804–1881)[1]

In 1914, the moment finally came for father to hand over to son. The scene was a successful shop in West London. But this familial transition was not without dispute. Against the wishes of his dad, the youngster made some changes that were revolutionary for the time. Shop staff were given rest breaks. The working day was shortened. Holidays were lengthened. Employee committees were established. A staff journal was created, complete with anonymous letters that challenged management practices.

The father was furious. But the son pressed on. Troubled by the fact that the family owners were paying themselves so much more than the average employee, he began reading widely. After a riding accident meant that he couldn't work for two years, the son had time to think even more deeply. Upon his return to the family firm, he took a radical leap of faith and decided to divide up the profits from the business each year and share them among all the staff.[2]

The John Lewis Partnership was formally established in 1920 when John Spedan Lewis created an employee benefit trust. Today, it is well known in the UK as a successful retailer that still divides up and shares its profits among all staff, who are known as partners. What is less well known is the central idea that guided Spedan Lewis in his model for the business: wellbeing.

Spedan Lewis described his vision for a firm "that will deliberately pursue happiness as diligently as plenty of communities pursue material wealth." He wrote: "there is an almost infinite variety of ways in which the management of an organisation like the Partnership can promote happiness. There is an almost infinite scope for imagination and energy."[3] Happiness was infused into the business. Wellbeing was the route to commercial success. Wealth through wellbeing was the critical insight that laid the foundations for John Lewis' success.

John Spedan Lewis took the usual step of creating a written constitution for the Partnership. This established the principle of profit-sharing among employees. Today, that constitution has an unequivocal commitment to wellbeing at its heart, declaring that: "The Partnership's ultimate purpose is the happiness of all its members, through their worthwhile and satisfying employment in a successful business".[4]

The model has paid off handsomely. John Lewis has grown from a single store to an £11 billion ($15 billion) business trading in 39 countries.[5] Around 70% of employees say that their job satisfies them – well in excess of industry averages. For the firm today, the wellbeing of all those affected by the company is not just something morally worthwhile that benefits others – it is viewed as intrinsically valuable to the organization itself.

New forms of capitalism

In the early twenty-first century, new ways of doing business are bubbling up across the world. Thousands of companies are taking steps to become more responsible and sustainable. New frameworks such as social enterprises and benefit corporations (B-Corps) are flourishing. Increasing numbers of investors are considering environmental, social and governance (ESG) factors. Slowly but surely, the foundations are being laid for a new form of capitalism.

Change has been spurred by corporate misdemeanours, cajoled by non-profits, led by some corporate pioneers, and championed by increasing numbers of consumers. Water targets, human rights codes, carbon strategies and anti-bribery training – the list of activities is long. Expectations of companies seem to increase by the day. But we need to pause and ask a fundamental question: what is it all for?

The old model held that the purpose of business was simply to satisfy shareholders.[6] The new approach has a bolder ambition: sustainable commerce that protects resources for future generations and shares value with society.[7] It is based on a stakeholder model, where the business considers groups such as employees, customers, suppliers, local communities, shareholders and all the other actors that are affected by the corporation. But if the end goal of the old model was profitable returns, what is our new destination? Preserving the environment and giving back to communities are worthy goals – but what is our aspiration for life? What does it all add up to?

The Wellbeing Purpose aspires to make life better. A Wellthy Company puts the *life satisfaction of stakeholders* at the heart of the firm. From the miner or farmer sweating at the top of the supply chain through to consumers exposed to branded advertising, each life that the business touches is considered and made more worthwhile.

For-profit entities must make a financial return. The happiness of shareholders – whether long-term pension funds or short-term hedge funds – is a core part of the purpose. But alongside wealth creation, the dream for business must be bolder.

A strategy that places wellbeing at its heart can return higher profits by means of enhancing life for all.

This chapter sets out a strategy for baking wellbeing into the core of the corporation. It outlines some practical steps that any organization can take to better more lives. This blueprint extends well beyond employment practices. It requires business model innovation, new metrics for success and a bold commitment to sell experiences that enhance life.

Jobs must have a purpose that makes employment worthwhile. Products need to be designed with wellbeing at their heart. Above all, the strategy needs to weave a consideration of human happiness throughout and across the business. We'll see how this strategic approach builds a self-sustaining business case through a virtuous circle of wellbeing. But every organization is different. The first step to shaping a winning strategy is to sketch the firm's unique imprint on life.

Mapping the wellbeing footprint

Imagine a business with an apparently fantastically happy story to tell. The farmers growing crops are provided with steady incomes and great working conditions. The manufacturing staff have the most wonderful career opportunities. Countless jobs are created in an extensive retail network, particularly in some of the poorest countries of the world. Community donations total tens of millions of dollars, all to amazing causes. It sounds like a dream, right? Then we come to the product, which has killed 100 million people in the twentieth century – more than all the deaths in World Wars I and II combined. This lethal consumable could eliminate another billion lives this century.[8]

Tobacco is a big killer, there's no doubt about that. Alongside fatalities, millions more live with ill health from puffing away and exposing others to second-hand smoke. The point here isn't about the rights and wrongs of the tobacco industry. The point is to illustrate the vital importance of adopting an expansive value chain approach to wellbeing. We cannot take a partial snapshot. After all, not all business influences on life are equal. The story of how companies can minimize harm and maximize happiness only makes sense if we begin with a wide-angle view.

The wellbeing footprint is the total picture of all the positive and negative effects of an organization along the value chain from suppliers to consumers. The starting point for any business should be to map its impacts on life, painting a picture of the credits and debits on this scorecard of humanity. The Wellbeing Purpose is about both eliminating the negatives and maximizing the positives to create a beneficial imprint.

Whenever a campaigning NGO tells a story of misery in the supply chain, or a journalist exposes advertising that is misleading, they are really questioning the wellbeing footprint. The critics are asking: is this business really making life better?

According to some, many of the heroes of capitalism – such as the fast-food and snack brands – are doing more damage than their smiling advertisements imply. Brands respond by saying that they provide choice and occasional treats. Tobacco and arms manufacturers often claim that the jobs they create justify their licence to operate. Calculating the wellbeing footprint can help to answer such challenges; it can flush out the truth behind claims. It can help to overcome some of the spin in responsible business and shed light on the real emotional and social influence of commerce.

Many of the benefits from wellbeing are often overlooked in traditional analyses of company impacts. For example, transportation companies such as airlines – frequently singled out for their environmental damage – create a lot of happiness through bringing people closer together. That doesn't excuse damaging the planet. But we need the whole picture. A good footprint analysis allows us to identify the negatives and weigh them up alongside the positives. It allows for a more complete analysis, a more informed conversation. Crucially, a balanced scorecard enables a more effective strategy for improvement.

Taking action

For most companies, the footprint varies considerably from person to person and place to place. The benefits for a vanilla bean farmer from a decent job will be much greater than the enjoyment that the shopper derives from eating vanilla ice cream. Starting with a solid grasp of the opportunity and risk profile allows us to ask the right questions. Where is the potential for life enhancement greatest? Where is the current frustration, anger and sadness most pertinent?

Mapping out the lives ("stakeholders," as the jargon goes) and how they are affected by business is only the starting point. Next, we need to apply the science. There are three areas to focus on, informed by the research that we examined in Chapter 2:

1   *Opportunity*: providing secure employment that contributes something to society.
2   *Vitality*: improving physical and mental health, self-esteem and nourishment.
3   *Connections*: fortifying relationships and improving safety and security.

Each step along the value chain can enhance or detract from the three vital ingredients of wellbeing. A Wellthy Company seeks to eliminate negatives and improve the positives in each area for as many stakeholder groups as possible.

Let's take another example to see how it works in practice. A large telecommunications company provides fixed-line telephone and internet across America. Current CSR activities involve reducing carbon emissions and employee volunteering. We map out the wellbeing footprint and discover two areas of utter misery for customers. Anonymous nuisance calls are distressing elderly and vulnerable customers. Engineers cancelling appointments are leaving a few very frustrated customers who have waited in and wasted time – yet still lack the digital connections that are vital to modern life. Both these issues are short-term irritations, not deep-rooted causes of unhappiness. But taken together, their impact appears relevant.

On the upside, the study reveals that major improvements to quality of life have come to a group of apprentices given their first jobs. Connecting the digitally isolated to high-speed networks has transformed how some people stay in touch with friends and family – and even improved health outcomes for some elderly customers. A sampling of the effects suggests life satisfaction has substantively been improved in terms of *opportunity*, *vitality* and *connections*.

Understanding the footprint can save millions of dollars in wasted effort. It can target improvements where lives are genuinely improved. It can attract and retain more customers. It can boost the top and bottom line. This is as much about refocusing ineffective expenditure as it is about targeting the right areas to better life for more people.

You may be wondering how companies can practically calculate their happiness footprint. Beyond employee satisfaction surveys, few organizations have successfully explored life enhancement studies. At a national level, much work has been done on measures of social progress that go beyond gross domestic product (GDP). Meanwhile, at an individual level, the surveys and methodologies we examined in Chapter 2 demonstrate how life satisfaction can be robustly measured for anyone.

Calculating a wellbeing footprint is no easy task. How might we work out the effects of a stable job or the joy derived from a technology that brings friends closer, or medicines that help us live longer? What about how a misguided advert chips away at self-esteem or worsens habits that make for poor health? Despite the scientific advances, we still can't put numbers on all the complex interactions that a business has. Typically, no single organization can take the credit or blame for the impacts of any one person's life.

Thirty years ago, the idea of environmental measurement seemed impossible. Now, some companies have highly detailed estimates of their credits and debits in natural capital accounting. Much work has been done in the field of socio-economic impact studies. We can calculate the business footprint on jobs, salaries, training and taxes. Even the indirect and knock-on impacts across communities can be worked out.

The same ideas must now be applied to the goal of life satisfaction. Some intuition is required. The Wellbeing Purpose is fundamentally about making a judgement as to what will do most to maximize happiness and minimise misery. We don't need a detailed statistical scorecard to take action. We just need some reasonable insight to focus our energy on the best ideas for bettering life.

Offsetting joy

Can one person's joy offset another's unhappiness? Jeremy Bentham, the founder of utilitarianism who we met in the Introduction, believed in the "greatest happiness of the greatest number." He imagined a world in which decisions were made for "the greatest possible quantity of happiness."[9] Ever since, there has been a major objection to his philosophy: it justifies bringing misery to the few if it results in happiness for the many. It's the total sum of pleasure that counts, according to utilitarians.

This objection is highly relevant for a Wellthy Company. Can we pollute a small village in order to bring life-saving clean water to a larger town? What if a brand enslaves hundreds of sweatshop labourers but produces cheap clothes for millions of consumers and profits for shareholders? These examples illustrate the fallacy of a "maximization" approach: it justifies victimizing a minority.

In the environmental arena, the parallel is something called offsetting. Burning fossil fuels can be mitigated by planting trees that soak up the equivalent emissions. Palm oil bought from dubious sources can be offset with squeaky clean certificates from more sustainable plantations. Offsetting has rightly come in for heavy criticism from environmentalists. Just because you grow flowers in one area, it doesn't make the stench disappear elsewhere.

The same applies to happiness: companies cannot offset their misery. A strategy for wellbeing cannot be about maximizing "pleasure," as utilitarians call it, at the expense of the few. Besides, the whole idea of seeking pleasure is misleading.

The Wellbeing Purpose is about life satisfaction. Happy hedonism is not the same thing as a well-rounded and fulfilling life. Knowledge and freedom may not create "pleasure," but they can make life feel better. As we've seen throughout this book, too many brands focus on short-term joy at the expense of long-term health and wellbeing. A focus on pleasure, not pain, justifies frivolous initiatives that do nothing to move the dial on life satisfaction.

Instead, a Wellthy Company eliminates the worst excesses of unhappiness and boosts the best impacts. Having sketched out the helicopter view, it's time to see how strategic decision-making can optimize wellbeing.

Restructuring and redundancies

In a world of rising populism, elites are facing growing dissatisfaction from the left-behinds of globalization. Jobs moving overseas, and a lack of new skills and opportunities, have been cited as major contributors in propelling Donald Trump into the White House[10] and Britain's vote to leave the European Union.[11]

By some alarming estimates, up to half of American jobs could be made redundant in the next 20 years due to the robotics revolution.[12] If these positions aren't replaced in new industries, then we could be in for a bleak future. Automation could fuel a jobless growth where unemployment rises and unhappiness spreads.

Throughout this book, we've seen how opportunities for employment can maximize happiness. Occupations provide a social setting, status, structure to the day and sense of meaning. Work is so vital to wellbeing that any job – no matter how bad – is normally better than none.[13] As the noted economist Lord Layard has written, "a bad job feels better than unemployment."[14] This is worth remembering when it comes to the hot topics of temporary workers and insecure work in the gig economy, as well as the debate over zero-hours contracts in the UK. That said, the evidence is clear that the more secure the work, and reliable the income, the better it is for wellbeing.[15]

The cardinal sin is making redundancies. Being out of work is the only major life event from which people don't fully recover within five years. The scars run deep and last long after re-employment.[16] In tough economic times, a business may reduce hours, move job locations, even cut pay. Each of these causes upheavals and upset. But none has as severe an impact as making someone redundant.

But what if restructuring is unavoidable? All industries face pressures over an economic cycle. Globalization and automation are continuing their steady march. The first thing to recognize is that the impact of unemployment varies by person and place. A young, skilled, mobile, urban professional will find it easier, quicker and less psychologically taxing to seek re-employment than a veteran of decades of work in a specialized role in manufacturing in a remote area. Unemployment is tragic for anyone, but it's much more devastating for some than others.

When restructuring is unavoidable, a Wellthy Company considers the effects of unemployment not just on the firm, but on each individual, their families and their communities. What are the chances of that person finding another job? What knock-on impacts might result from a redundancy? Let's be honest: these considerations are not fashionable when it comes to human resources. The focus is on the business needs, the individual's job spec and a heavy dose of legal advice. But if we want companies to be a force for life enhancement, we simply cannot take a narrow view of something as vital as jobs.

Alongside a job, a Wellthy Company considers how work affects the other two vital ingredients of life: *vitality* and *connections*. Dignity, respect and support for mental and physical health complement the opportunities at a Wellthy Company. Giving staff more time, flexibility and autonomy creates happier employees with better work–life balance.

But the company's employment practices are only one piece of the puzzle. The biggest impacts on *vitality* and *connections* typically lie beyond the production lines and office cubicles. This requires developing and selling products and services that make life better for everyone. In order to deliver on this aspiration, the corporation must look purposefully at opportunities for innovation.

Innovation for wellbeing

A Wellthy Company delivers groundbreaking innovations that diffuse happiness across society. Quality of life is improved faster by baking social outcomes into the innovation processes and business model. What discoveries might improve mental health for customers? What inventive new delivery models could create more meaningful work? How might a new service build stronger connections between families? A Wellthy Company sets out to discover how to make life healthier, create more human relationships and give everyone more opportunities in life.

A pioneering approach to innovation requires a long-term outlook and an open mind. When it comes to products, a Wellthy Company invests in a research and development pipeline with a bold ambition: to boost the quality of life of those who buy, use and are affected by the portfolio.[17] Some creations directly raise wellbeing, such as medicines and nourishing foods. Some products undermine happiness, by providing new forms of addictive harm. As we saw in Chapter 6, certain goods require a balance: alcohol, gambling and consumer credit, for example, may be enjoyable and useful in the right quantities. But taken to excess, or by vulnerable groups, they can have the opposite effect. A Wellthy Company innovates the design, distribution and marketing to ensure that the right products get to the right people in the right quantities at the right time.

There's been a lot of excitement in recent years about eco-innovation. Consumer goods giants such as P&G, L'Oréal and Unilever are adding an environmental lens to their R&D pipelines. By recalibrating their development processes, they are reducing greenhouse gases in supply chains and manufacturing, creating less waste and helping us to use less water when we wash, cook and clean at home.

Why not apply the same ideas to quality of life? Design for wellbeing is currently a small field with huge potential. Instead of environmental profiling, a Wellthy Company uses the science of happiness as the lens for innovation. How can users have their lives made richer as a result of a product?

There are multiple layers to enhancing life through a brand. On the surface, there are aesthetics. Beautiful design can bring a smile. A good architect can promote social interactions through clever communal spaces, staircases, corridors and use of light. We can innovate games that bring laughter and amusement – and perhaps learn something worthwhile or improve lifestyle behaviours at the same time.

We might design to help people to reach personal goals, whether that's great food for a better diet, trainers to run a marathon or an instrument to learn music.[18] Brands can be a powerful force for strengthening personal identity. When we feel part of something bigger, we feel happier. Hobbyists can be given opportunities to share their passion with like-minded collectors,[19] or online communities developed to provide support to those at risk of isolation.

To maximize the wellbeing footprint, a Wellthy Company invests in solutions that raise quality of life not just for consumers, but also employees, suppliers and their families, friends and neighbours. M. Joseph Sirgy and Dong-Jin Lee, two experts in ethical marketing, use the example of car safety. A wellbeing approach goes well beyond regulatory requirements and consumer preferences. We factor in the safety, noise and pollution concerns of passengers, pedestrians, mechanics and neighbours.[20] This whole-life approach to innovation can transform how we think about what society values from products and services.

New models for a happier business

Let's be honest: product innovation is just tinkering at the edges. It can only get us so far. If our purpose is for a truly life-changing impact on the world, we must raise our aspirations for innovation. We must harness the full power of business by rethinking the very structure of commerce.

A business model is a story about how a company makes money. It includes all the activities associated with making something: design, purchase of raw materials, and manufacture. It also includes selling: identifying and reaching customers, and distributing the product or delivering the service.[21]

Unpacking the business model opens up countless new opportunities for enhancing life. Let's start with who can buy the brand. It's no good having life-fulfilling products if we can't bring the benefits to those that need them the most. Can the chronically obese afford your healthier food? Can the vulnerable or isolated access technology that links them to others? A Wellthy Company seeks to put life-changing products and services into the hands of as many people who might benefit as possible.[22]

This is an area that is very familiar to pharmaceutical firms. Access to medicines is a crucial issue when it comes to healthcare's social impact. Financial services also promote access to affordable credit and savings accounts to those who might otherwise lack them. Food businesses can try to increase the uptake of their most nutritionally beneficial products.

On every MBA course, you are taught that revenues are made up of price and sales volume. Lower the price, and you need to increase the volume to hit the same revenue total. A Wellthy Company makes socially beneficial products available at a low price and a high volume. That doesn't mean making less money if the sales strategy is bold enough and the cost base is managed. In the new wellbeing economy, we can expect more companies to report on the *quantity* of good products and services sold (not just their value), and the number of lives that have been improved as a result.[23]

The ideas of access and availability can also extend to job opportunities. It's no good having worthwhile occupations if candidates who might benefit the most can't work for you. Can the out-of-work mum with the right qualifications realistically get a job at your firm? Can the best suppliers, even if they are small-scale entrepreneurs, ever land a contract with you?

A business model for happiness requires a redesign of distribution networks. Involving new groups in the transportation and sale of a product can raise wellbeing further. Small retailers and entrepreneurial distributors can widen access to a product and benefit from the work too. For example, Unilever's Shakti scheme has created jobs for nearly 70,000 women selling household products such as soap to over 4 million rural households in India.[24]

The wellbeing model is radically different from a business-as-usual approach. It involves making a series of decisions to put the happiness of all stakeholders – employees, consumers, suppliers, communities, shareholders – at the heart of the business model. It requires taking decisions at a strategic level to prioritize quality of life as a route to growth.

For example, if estimates indicate that sourcing materials from a poorer women's cooperative would have a much larger impact on wellbeing than business as usual, or a wider distribution model could provide more jobs and increase access, then change is embraced. All this can make for a happier, healthier network of people, more dedicated and loyal staff and customers, and so drive shareholder value.

Delivering happiness

Zappos is an online store with a phenomenal growth story. The retailer of shoes and clothes began life in 1999. Despite investing little into advertising, it rapidly became a household name in America. Just 10 years after it was founded, Amazon bought the business in a deal valued at $1.2 billion. But this isn't an ordinary tale of start-up success.

The science of wellbeing was the inspiration for the firm's growth. Tony Hsieh, the charismatic founder, read up on happiness. He quickly realized some lucrative implications for his start-up. One key insight was that happiness stems from strong relationships between people. He realized that a focus on wellbeing could ensure that customers wanted to buy from Zappos time and again. So, he set the corporate purpose as "Delivering Happiness to the World" and created a unique culture to win the trust of customers.

In his book *Delivering Happiness*, Hsieh explained:

> If the ultimate goal is happiness, then why wouldn't it make sense for you to study and learn more about the science of happiness . . . ? . . . How much happier could your customers and employees be if you applied the knowledge to your company? How much healthier would your business be as a result?[25]

Drawing inspiration from this purpose, Hsieh created a firm that was intensely focused on customer care. Rather than the standard delivery times, Zappos introduced free upgrades to overnight shipping. The aim was to not just satisfy those who bought from the store, but truly delight them. A bunch of flowers might arrive out of the blue to thank someone for buying shoes. All this is part of what Hsieh calls a "happiness framework" and a "higher purpose" of "being part of something bigger."

Zappos shows how creating positive emotions can build confidence in the brand and a loyal fan base of customers who repeat-purchase and recommend the company. While Zappos focused primarily on delighting customers and employees, the opportunity of a true purpose is to embed it in into the DNA of a firm.

True purpose is a virtuous circle

For many businesses today, talk of purpose and happiness is only skin-deep. Scratch beneath the surface of many smiling brands and you'll find fleeting joy, fuelled by stressed employees and neglected communities. That type of happiness isn't sustainable. It won't create real benefits for anyone.

All too often, purpose boils down to a fancy campaign that's as fickle as it is short-lived. That's not strategic. True purpose reshapes the firm. True purpose moulds the corporate values and affects the day-to-day behaviours of employees. True purpose changes the products and services that are innovated for customers. True purpose recalibrates the business model: transforming how value is created and shared among stakeholders.

The Wellbeing Purpose creates a self-sustaining, virtuous circle that reaches broadly and deeply into the firm to change society. If you take too narrow a view of the value chain – only employees, for example – you miss the wider benefits. A broader view opens up opportunities for cross-pollination. A rising tide lifts all the boats: suppliers, customers, employees and local communities all making each other feel better about life. This approach reaps dividends because happiness is infectious. Positive feelings in one group – such as employees – rub off on to others, especially customers.[26]

Similarly, if you take too shallow a stab at happiness – only scratching the surface of short-term feelings – it won't affect real change. The substantive transformation of life requires considering the different domains: health, family, relationships, leisure time and work. The field of view for business cannot be limited to the workplace.

This depth can build momentum. For any individual, raising their happiness in one area – such as through a fulfilling occupation – can improve the others. A stimulating job and good work–life balance can strengthen relationships at home. Improving a supplier's health may make them more productive in their free time. Fundamentally, the business case from a more productive workforce, engaged suppliers and more loyal customers only makes sense if the ambition is to really make a genuine contribution to making life feel better.

By reaching broadly (multiple stakeholders) and deeply (substantive life satisfaction), the Wellbeing Purpose builds a virtuous circle. Studies show that the happier people are, the more successful they become.[27] Happier workers tend to excel with improved self-esteem and a positive outlook that raises optimism, confidence and productivity.[28] In turn, this pool of success can raise happiness for others further.[29] More stakeholders will benefit. The transformative potential of the Wellbeing Purpose makes most sense when it is ambitious.

In the long run, the Wellbeing Purpose should make one final group happier: shareholders. Studies show that companies with more satisfied customers perform better financially.[30] Healthier, happier customers tend to live longer (a bigger market) and return time and again to favoured brands. Happier workers are more productive, less sick, more loyal, less absent, more creative, more successful and more collaborative.[31] That's why organizations with happier, more engaged staff typically have share prices that rise faster than their competitors.[32]

The Wellbeing Purpose can deliver wellbeing and wealth. Life enhancement can fuel growth. But is selling more and more stuff really going to improve life? If you are a healthcare or wholesome foods business, the answer might be yes. More sales should result in better lives. But for everyone else, doesn't the research show that selling more stuff is making everyone more miserable?

Jumping off the hedonic treadmill

Throughout this book, we've seen how material things – such as big pay cheques, big cars, big houses – do little for happiness. The research is pretty categorical: buying more stuff – gadgets, foods, vehicles, housing and even medical care – is not significantly associated with increased happiness.[33] We are buying things that companies produce that really do very little to improve quality of life. This is a tough message for many brands to accept. But if we are serious about the science, we need to wake up to this reality. We cannot afford to ignore the challenge of consumption.

One of the sacred cows of capitalism is growth. As a society, we need to create, sell and consume more and more in order to continue the steady march of progress. This is the reason why there is so much obsession with quarterly growth figures. For many businesses, alarm bells go off (and heads sometimes roll) when fewer units are shifted in one quarter than the previous one.

Psychologists call this the hedonic treadmill. It's hedonic because, as individuals, we want the bigger car. It's a treadmill because, as we become aware of better choices and then experience that car, we quickly adapt. Our happiness reverts to its prior state; consumption efforts are futile.

Environmentalists have long challenged the premise of growth. Writers such as Tim Jackson have argued that we simply cannot go on consuming at our current rate and leave the planet in a sustainable state. Growth itself is seen as the problem.[34]

The science of wellbeing casts a new light on this thorny topic. We should question the assumption that greater happiness will come from the next product bought or the next goal accomplished.[35] The truth is that selling that next phone or pair of jeans to someone who already has one won't increase the sum of human happiness. Essential purchases of soap, toothpaste, food or medicines may be the exception. But for everyone else, what benefit does consumption really bring?

Leadership in the wellbeing economy will question the fundamentals of materialistic growth. Many businesses won't be comfortable with this. It's taken many years, but some leading energy companies now accept the need to sell less high-carbon energy – but still make a profit. How are they going to do that? By shifting the business model away from products and selling *services*.

Businesses can grow revenues and increase profits through selling experiences, not just more units. This approach will have both environmental as well as wellbeing benefits. It's rarely the products that affect our happiness. It's what we do with them that counts.

A Wellthy Company sells what are called experiential products. An enjoyable meal, movie, trip or game creates joy in the instant, supports relationships and creates memories. The best experiences for happiness are those that we never fully adapt to and never take for granted. Spending money on leisure – often shared with others – is one of the few purchases that research suggests does raise happiness.[36]

A second route to wellbeing is spending money on others. One neat study illustrates the point. Participants were asked to recall a time that they'd spent cash on someone else. A control group were asked to think of a time they'd splashed out on themselves. After a little consideration, participants were asked whether they'd like to spend some imaginary cash on a purchase for a loved one or themselves. Those who'd recalled spending money on someone else were much more likely to want to do so again.[37] Could brands do more to share their benefits by encouraging gifting?

Spending our money on experiences and on other people is all part of a wider issue about wealth. A Wellthy Company is not about increasing material affluence. It's about increasing *opportunities*, *vitality* and *connections*. That's a big mindset shift. The psychologist and author Tim Kasser puts this succinctly:

> Given that increases in wealth are not associated with increases in happiness, is it ethical for a business to single-mindedly pursue profit? Given that financial rewards can undermine the intrinsic motivation and enjoyment that comes from pursuing activities (including work activities), is it ethical for companies to reward employees primarily with financial raises and bonuses? Also, given that people experience lower well-being when they strongly value materialistic goals, is it ethical to . . . suggest that companies place pay at the center of their business culture and celebrate competition and wealth?[38]

Some argue that the very idea of a for-profit business is incompatible with wellbeing. Business, growth and wealth seem to jar with what the science indicates will make us content. But profit per se is not bad. There is no reason why an organization that creates wealth and shares it widely should not also increase life satisfaction. Indeed, profits enable a business to scale and so benefit more people. It's *how* that wealth is generated and distributed that we should be concerned with.

We need to reconsider what we are placing value on as a society. Business plays a major part in this, shaping culture and expectations through employment, products and marketing. The solution is surely to strike a balance. Wealth matters. But we must not value it to the detriment of things such as friendships, families, leisure time and good health.

The sceptics' challenge

Ever since governments began exploring gross national happiness, three problems have cropped up. The first concerns measurement. Do we really know what makes people happy? The last 20 years of research has answered this convincingly. As outlined in Chapter 2, the science is robust. The statistics, in aggregate, paint a compelling picture of what makes life better. The idea that we simply don't know what makes us content – or how to calculate it for any person or business – is no longer true. What we now need is for more businesses to link their actions to the empirical research. In the words of happiness expert Lord Layard, we need more organizations to measure "what people feel, not what people think they feel."[39]

The second issue concerns the destination. Is happiness really an appropriate end goal? Shouldn't governments just grow the economy, deliver public services and provide a safety net? Shouldn't companies just crack on with wealth generation while improving working conditions, product quality and the environment? This argument suggests it's better to focus on the *means* to ends rather than the ends in themselves.[40]

In any business environment, investment is always finite. Choices need to be made. Without a clear end goal, managers risk being buffeted by whichever wind blows that day. Is it better to invest half a million dollars in pay rises for staff, better training or more holidays? Asking employees would suggest the former, management consultants might advise the second, but the science of wellbeing would suggest giving more time and flexibility is the fastest route to raising quality of life.

Life satisfaction is the only goal that, to restate the words of Aristotle that began this book, "is absolutely final. For we always choose it for the sake of itself and never for the sake of something else."[41] The ultimate objective for each of us as individuals is to lead a happy and fulfilled life. It is surely the only logical end goal for responsible business too.

A final critique of wellbeing is that it smacks of paternalism. Some have questioned whether we really want governments trying to make us happy. The same concern has been levelled at business by William Davies in a book called *The Happiness Industry*.[42] The critics claim that we don't want corporates invading our lives and second-guessing what makes us happy.

This is an argument for a pre-industrial society of cottage industries and rural fiefdoms. In the real world, big business already decides the daily chores of billions at work, the products in our stores and the advertising messages that saturate our lives.

The anti-capitalists say that this is exactly what we need to stop. Despite centuries of trying, those against the march of modernization, commercialism and globalization have failed to reverse the trends. Despite recent predictions of a retreat of globalization,[43] there is little evidence of a serious dent to these mega-forces. Rather than swimming against the tide, companies can help to reorient our direction of travel. Rather than trying to overthrow capitalism, we need to focus on building a better economy that improves life for billions of people.

Happiness does not limit life; it enables it. As the seventeenth-century philosopher John Locke put it, focusing on a full and happy life is the surest route to freedom. It is the "imaginary" joy of fleeting, false promises that we should be wary of.[44] Businesses that enable more people to lead a satisfied existence are not tricking anyone. Changing products and marketing messages to nudge us towards healthy behaviours, for example, is not sinister. It's the fake claims by brands based on pseudoscience that we should be worried about. The Wellbeing Purpose should tap into real needs and genuine desires – based on what we know raises life satisfaction. Far from limiting opportunities, we should celebrate this as liberating life to be lived to the full.

The real question is not whether wellbeing should be the goal for business. I believe there is no more logical purpose for brands that care about their role in the world. Instead, we should ask: how far are we prepared to let companies go? How ambitious do we want to be?

Let's go back to that example of pay versus holidays. Most employees don't ask for less pay and more time off. But the science is categorical in showing that for most people, more free time (for less pay) would make us happier. Should companies just make the decision for us? The academics Daniel Kahneman and Richard Thaler have suggested exactly this. They propose that managers should add vacation time, and reduce pay accordingly, while giving staff the option to "work those extra vacation days" for more pay should they so wish.[45]

An opt-out system that nudges staff to take more holidays and cuts their pay in return is certainly radical. If implemented by a large multinational, it would no doubt be met with howls of protest from the media and unions. The limits of corporate nudging for wellbeing need to be debated and an appropriate role for companies found. The science on what's in our long-term interests often jars with individual instincts. It's in these situations that some of the most challenging choices emerge.

Realizing the Wellbeing Purpose is no easy task. The right approach will not always be clear. We need more companies to embrace the ideas and apply their skills in consumer research and marketing to better understand what works. Equally, we should be honest that some investments that boost wellbeing may see higher costs and foregone revenues in the short term – such as fewer Happy Meals sold to kids. The business case may not always work. But when it does, companies can find higher levels of trust, new revenue opportunities, more customer loyalty, higher productivity, less regulatory risk and more brand credibility in the long run.

Of course, companies cannot do everything. Governments are vital to creating the facilitating environment that supports a wellbeing economy. Without regulation to shift our economies away from short-termism, many of the promises of the Wellthy Company will be harder to achieve. Tax breaks for products that improve life, regulations to support flexible working and aggressively pursuing the corporate cheats that make life miserable will speed up the shift. At the same time, we must recognize that even with supportive governments and bold businesses, it may not be possible to make everyone happy. Genes play a vital role in our outlook; much of the variation in wellbeing could be down to our inherited personality.[46]

The emotional economy of the future

What role do we want companies to play in our world? The answer to this question has changed in recent times. Once it was about philanthropy – giving something back to communities. Next came corporate social responsibility – doing less bad. Then we had "sustainable business" and "shared value" – delivering environmental and social improvements to better our planet.

The role of people and their betterment has been badly overlooked. What is the shared aspiration that we have for life? The future of responsible and sustainable business must be to examine and improve life satisfaction. This is about creating a more human form of capitalism. There is inherent value to life that we must never take for granted.[47] For companies bold enough to seize the initiative, wellbeing can be a powerful differentiator in hiring and motivating staff, pioneering products, getting the most out of business partners, and forging relationships with customers and communities.

The Wellbeing Purpose is about putting life at the heart of the business model. But it's a far cry from just adding "people" to a CSR plan next to "planet" and "profit." It's not about short-lived initiatives to get employees cycling to work – worse still those marketing gimmicks about the joy of jolly brands.

The Wellbeing Purpose has an aspiration to make life more fulfilling for the 2.2 billion people who wake up each day and, if asked, would rate their very existence *less* than 5 out of 10.[48] It's about creating more reasons for everyone to feel that living has meaning, and that they have a purpose in life.

If we get this right, the future for business could be an incredibly exciting and rewarding one. As the happiness economy develops, we can expect to see more companies measure and value wellbeing.[49] I hope that we will see some pioneers assessing the dollar per happiness impact of their activities – a social return on investment that assesses life enhancement. We might one day see the world's first Wellbeing Profit and Loss Account – detailing estimates of the credits and debits on a living scorecard.

Certifications such as fair trade focus on supplier conditions. Many countries mandate nutritional labelling to help us make informed decisions about what we eat and drink. Perhaps in the future we could see products stamped[50] that are "good for life" from supplier inputs to consumption impacts. With the right data, radical claims could be made by experiential brands that are "scientifically proven" to help us feel better. Who wouldn't want to buy into that?

Business is ultimately about generating a return for shareholders through creating value for customers. A better understanding of what really creates human value – a sustained, positive, emotional response – must make brands more successful. Estimating how products and services improve life for those buying and using them will spur wealth creation. If this is done well, then we must expect socially responsible investors of the future to add a consideration of life betterment to their screens for the most profitable, long-term holdings.

Our world has never been more in need of a happiness agenda. The size and power of modern corporations gives them a unique responsibility to minimize suffering and better life. The future will not be about whether your business is zero-carbon, or ethical, or sustainable. It will be about whether you are raising life satisfaction – whether you have a positive wellbeing footprint.

If you pick up many self-help books, they will tell you that happiness cannot be willed. It is a journey, not a destination. As the Chinese Philosopher Zhuang Zhou put it in the fourth century, "Happiness is the absence of striving for happiness." The big difference with running an organization is that we *can* will the end we desire. That's what leadership is about – setting the vision and galvanizing others to deliver meaningful change. The evidence is there, staring us in the face: wellbeing can make us all happier and business more profitable. Any organization can make wellbeing its purpose. Any company can act today to raise life satisfaction. A world where business genuinely makes life better for more of humanity is something we could all be happier for.

Notes

1 Cited in Edwards, T. (2015). *The New Dictionary of Thoughts*. San Francisco, CA: Ravenio Books.
2 Salaman, G. & Storey, J. (2016). *A Better Way of Doing Business? Lessons from the John Lewis Partnership*. Oxford: Oxford University Press.
3 Lewis, J. S. (1948). *Partership for All*. London: The Kerr Cross Publishing Co Ltd.
4 John Lewis Partnership (2018). *The Constitution of the John Lewis Partnership*. London: John Lewis Partnership. Retrieved 8 June 2018, from www.johnlewispartnership. co.uk/content/dam/cws/pdfs/about-us/our-constitution/john-lewis-partnership-constitution.pdf.
5 John Lewis Partnership (2017). *Unaudited Results for 52 Weeks Ended 28 January 2017*. London: John Lewis Partnership.
6 Most famously by Friedman, M. (1970). The social responsibility of business is to increase its profits. *New York Times Magazine*, 13 September.
7 Porter, M. E. & Kramer, M. R. (2011). The big idea: creating shared value. *Harvard Business Review*, 89(1–2), 62–77.
8 World Health Organization (2008). *WHO Report on the Global Tobacco Epidemic*. Geneva: World Health Organization.
9 Bentham, J. (1823). *A Fragment on Government: And an Introduction to the Principles of Morals and Legislation*. London: W. Pickering.
10 For example, see Spangler, T. D. (2017). The Rust Belt gave Trump victory, now they want jobs in return. *USA Today*, 18 January.
11 Goodwin, M. & Heath, O. (2016). Brexit vote explained: poverty, low skills and lack of opportunities. *Solve UK Poverty* (Series), 31 August. London: Joseph Rowntree Foundation.
12 Frey, C. B. & Osborne, M. A. (2013). *The Future of Employment: How Susceptible Are Jobs to Computerisation?* Oxford: Oxford Martin School.
13 Ibid.
14 Layard, R. (2004). *Good Jobs and Bad Jobs*. Paper presented to the OECD Ministers of Employment, 29 September 2003.
15 For data supporting this, see New Economics Foundation (2014). *Wellbeing at Work: A Review of the Literature*. London: New Economics Foundation.
16 O'Donnell, G., Deaton, A., Durand, M., Halpern, D. & Layard, R. (2014). *Wellbeing and Policy*. London: Legatum Institute.
17 Sirgy, M. J. & Lee, D. J. (2008). Well-being marketing: an ethical business philosophy for consumer goods firms. *Journal of Business Ethics*, 77(4), 377–403.
18 Desmet, P. M. & Pohlmeyer, A. E. (2013). Positive design: an introduction to design for subjective well-being. *International Journal of Design*, 7(3), 5–19.
19 Sirgy, M. J. & Lee, D. J. (2008). Well-being marketing: an ethical business philosophy for consumer goods firms. *Journal of Business Ethics*, 77(4), 377–403.
20 Ibid.
21 Magretta, J. (2002). Why business models matter. *Harvard Business Review*, 80(5), 86–92.
22 Sirgy, M. J. & Lee, D. J. (2008). Well-being marketing: an ethical business philosophy for consumer goods firms. *Journal of Business Ethics*, 77(4), 377–403.
23 Sirgy, M. J. (2001). *Handbook of Quality-of-Life Research: An Ethical Marketing Perspective* (Vol. 8). Dordrecht: Kluwer Academic Publishers.

24 Hindustan Unilever (2017). *Enhancing Livelihoods through Project Shakti*. Retrieved 14 June 2017, from www.hul.co.in/sustainable-living/case-studies/enhancing-livelihoods-through-project-shakti.html.

25 Hsieh, T. (2010). *Delivering Happiness: A Path to Profits, Passion, and Purpose*. London: Hachette UK.

26 Heskett, J. L. & Schlesinger, L. A. (1994). Putting the service-profit chain to work. *Harvard Business Review*, *72*(2), 164–174.

27 Lyubomirsky, S., King, L. & Diener, E. (2005). The benefits of frequent positive affect: does happiness lead to success? *Psychological Bulletin*, *131*(6), 803–855.

28 Graham, C. (2012). *Happiness around the World: The Paradox of Happy Peasants and Miserable Millionaires*. Oxford: Oxford University Press.

29 Lyubomirsky, S., King, L. & Diener, E. (2005). The benefits of frequent positive affect: does happiness lead to success? *Psychological Bulletin*, *131*(6), 803–855.

30 Hart, C. W. (2007). Beating the market with customer satisfaction. *Harvard Business Review*, *85*(3), 30–32.

31 Bao, K. J. & Lyubomirsky, S. (2013). The rewards of happiness. In S. A. David, I. Boniwell & A. C. Ayers (eds.), *The Oxford Handbook of Happiness* (pp. 119–133). Oxford: Oxford University Press; Pavot, W. & Diener, E. (2013). Happiness experienced: the science of subjective well-being. In S. A. David, I. Boniwell & A. C. Ayers (eds.), *The Oxford Handbook of Happiness* (pp. 134–151). Oxford: Oxford University Press.

32 Edmans, A. (2012). The link between job satisfaction and firm value, with implications for corporate social responsibility. *The Academy of Management Perspectives*, *26*(4), 1–19; Edmans, A., Li, L. & Zhang, C. (2014). *Employee Satisfaction, Labor Market Flexibility, and Stock Returns around the World* (No. w20300). Cambridge, MA: National Bureau of Economic Research.

33 DeLeire, T. & Kalil, A. (2010). Does consumption buy happiness? Evidence from the United States. *International Review of Economics*, *57*(2), 163–176.

34 Jackson, T. (2011). *Prosperity without Growth: Economics for a Finite Planet*. New York: Routledge.

35 Diener, E., Lucas, R. E. & Scollon, C. N. (2006). Beyond the hedonic treadmill: revising the adaptation theory of well-being. *American Psychologist*, *61*(4), 305–314.

36 DeLeire, T. & Kalil, A. (2010). Does consumption buy happiness? Evidence from the United States. *International Review of Economics*, *57*(2), 163–176.

37 Aknin, L. B., Dunn, E. W. & Norton, M. I. (2012). Happiness runs in a circular motion: evidence for a positive feedback loop between prosocial spending and happiness. *Journal of Happiness Studies*, *13*(2), 347–355.

38 Kasser, T. & Sheldon, K. M. (2009). Time affluence as a path toward personal happiness and ethical business practice: empirical evidence from four studies. *Journal of Business Ethics*, *84*(2), 243–255.

39 Layard, R. (2011). *Happiness: Lessons from a New Science*. London: Penguin, p. 121.

40 Thin, N. (2012). *Social Happiness: Theory into Policy and Practice*. Bristol: Policy Press, p. 212.

41 Aristotle, *Nicomachean Ethics*, Book I, Chapter 4.

42 Davies, W. (2015). *The Happiness Industry: How the Government and Big Business Sold Us Well-Being*. London: Verso Books.

43 For example, Emmott, B. (2017). The fate of the West: the battle to save the world's most successful political idea. *The Economist*.

44 Locke, J. (1836). *An Essay Concerning Human Understanding*. London: T. Tegg & Son.

45 Kahneman, D. & Thaler, R. H. (2006). Anomalies: utility maximization and experienced utility. *Journal of Economic Perspectives*, *20*(1), 221–234.

46 By some estimates, between 50% and 80% could be down to genes. See Lykken, D. & Tellegen, A. (1996). Happiness is a stochastic phenomenon. *Psychological Science*, *7*(3), 186–189.

47 Kant, I. (1991). *The Metaphysics of Morals*, M. Gregor (trans.). New York: Cambridge University Press.

48 Calculated from data appendices to Helliwell, J. F., Layard, R. and Sachs, J. (eds.) (2015). *World Happiness Report 2015*. New York: Sustainable Development Solutions Network.

49 Elkington, J. & Zeitz, J. (2014). *The Breakthrough Challenge: 10 Ways to Connect Today's Profits with Tomorrow's Bottom Line*. London: John Wiley & Sons.

50 Wallman, J. (2015). *Stuffocation: Why We've Had Enough of Stuff and Need Experience More Than Ever*. New York: Spiegel & Grau.

Acknowledgements

I am indebted to many friends, family, colleagues and clients who have provided inspiration for this book. The kernel of an idea was planted at Forum for the Future, where, alongside James Goodman and David Bent, I developed a scenario called Redefining Progress as part of Climate Futures 2030. The project was supported by HP Labs with Chris Preist and Paul Shabajee.

Mike Tuffrey, co-founder of Corporate Citizenship, has been instrumental in shaping many of my views over the years, as well as drafts of this book. My sister, Katie Hardyment (formerly of Good Business), provided invaluable input through detailed comments on my manuscript. Special mention should also go to the team at Unilever, led by Karen Hamilton, whose projects over many years have furnished me with countless ideas that have ended up scattered throughout this book.

Christina Hardyment, Cecilia Law, Karin Laljani and Jon Leach also deserve a mention, as well as the support and guidance provided to a first-time author by Judith Lorton and Rebecca Marsh at Taylor & Francis and Andrew Craddock for his eagle-eyed copy-editing.

Finally, my family. To my wife, Kate, for her patience over the five years it's taken from idea to publication. And my daughter, Ada, to whom this book is dedicated, whose birth brought me the space to start thinking – as well as great personal happiness.

Index